Eliza Brown Chase

Over the Border

Acadia

Eliza Brown Chase

Over the Border
Acadia

ISBN/EAN: 9783337340674

Printed in Europe, USA, Canada, Australia, Japan

Cover: Foto ©Thomas Meinert / pixelio.de

More available books at **www.hansebooks.com**

OVER THE BORDER

ACADIA

THE HOME OF "EVANGELINE"

BY

𝔚ith Illustrations in 𝔥eliotype from 𝔚ater-𝔠olor 𝔖ketches
BY THE AUTHOR

"Here lies the East: does not the day break here?"
JULIUS CÆSAR, II. i.

BOSTON
JAMES R. OSGOOD AND COMPANY
1884

CONTENTS.

	PAGE
THE BAY OF FUNDY	19
THE BASIN OF MINAS	29
PORT ROYAL	45
ANNAPOLIS	61
DIGBY	113
HALIFAX	123
GRAND PRÉ	135
CLARE	153
L'ISLE DES MONTS DESERTS	183

ILLUSTRATIONS.

Cape Blomidon, Basin of Minas.

Old Friends' Almshouse, Philadelphia.

Cape Sharp, Cape Split, and Partridge Island, Bay of Fundy.

The Old Block House, Ancient Archway in the Fort, Annapolis.

Great St. George's Street, Annapolis.

The Digby Gap.

Grand Pré.

Map of the Acadian Region.

CHRONOLOGY.

DATE.		PAGE
1604.	De Monts's first landing on Eastern coast (May 16)	40
1604.	De Monts and suite arrive at Port Royal (about June 1)	41
1606.	De Monts returns from France with supplies for his colony	47
1606.	Port Royal abandoned	48
1610.	Return of De Poutrincourt	48
1612.	Jesuit priests sent out from France. (Founding of St. Sauveur colony at Mt. Desert)	49
1613.	Destruction of Port Royal by Argall (after breaking up settlement at Mt. Desert)	50
1628.	Scotch colony broken up at Port Royal	53
1634.	Port Royal held by French under De Razilly	53
1647.	Feud between La Tour and D'Aulnay	53
1654.	Port Royal under Le Borgne yields to English	55
1684.	Incursions of pirates	55
1690.	Sir Wm. Phipps captures and pillages Port Royal	55
1691.	Port Royal held by French under De Villebon	55
1707.	Unsuccessfully besieged	55

CHRONOLOGY.

DATE.		PAGE
1710.	Bombarded by seven English ships; the fort yields; name changed to Annapolis Royal	56
1713.	Treaty of Utrecht, ceding Acadia to the English	140
1727, 1728.	Oath of allegiance exempting French Acadians from taking arms against France	140
1744.	Port Royal bombarded and besieged three months	56
1745.	De Ramezay's unsuccessful attack	57
1755.	Forts Beau-Séjour and Gaspereau taken by Moncton	143
1755.	Dispersion of the "Neutrals"	143–148
1763.	Return of exiles, and founding of coast settlements. Treaty between France and England	154
1781.	Annapolis Royal surprised and taken by two war ships	57
1850.	Last occupation (by military force) of old fort at Annapolis	57

INTRODUCTION.

In the rooms of the Historical Society, in Boston, hangs a portrait of a distinguished-looking person in quaint but handsome costume of antique style. The gold-embroidered coat, long vest with large and numerous buttons, elegant cocked hat under the arm, voluminous white scarf and powdered peruke, combine to form picturesque attire which is most becoming to the gentleman therein depicted, and attract attention to the genial countenance, causing the visitor to wonder who this can be, so elaborately presented to the gaze.

A physiognomist would not decide upon such representation as a "counterfeit presentment" of the tyrannical leader of the expedition which enforced the cruel edict of exile, —

"In the Acadian land, on the shores of the Basin of Minas;
  where
Distant, secluded, still, the little village of Grand Pré
Lay in the fruitful valley."

Yet this is Lieutenant-Colonel John Winslow, great-grandson of one of the founders of the Plymouth Settlement. Could *he* forget that his ancestors fled from persecution, and came to this country to find peaceful homes?

It was not his place to make reply, or reason why when receiving orders, however; and it seems that the task imposed was a distasteful one; as, at the time of the banishment, he earnestly expressed the desire " to be rid of the worst piece of service " he " ever was in."

He said also of the unhappy people at that time, " It hurts me to hear their weeping and wailing." So we conclude that the pleasant face did not belie the heart which it mirrored.

It is a singular coincidence that, for being hostile to their country at the time of the Revolution, his own family were driven into exile twenty years after the deportation of the unhappy French people.

Have not even the most prosaic among us some love of poesy, though unacknowledged? And who, in romantic youth or sober age, has not been touched by the tragic story of the dispersion of the people who

> " dwelt together in love, those simple Acadian farmers,—
> Dwelt in the love of God and of man. Alike were they free from
> Fear, that reigns with the tyrant, and envy, the vice of republics.

Neither locks had they to their doors, nor bars to their windows;
But their dwellings were open as day and the hearts of their owners;
There the richest was poor, and the poorest lived in abundance."

Of the name Acadia, Principal Dawson says in " Canadian Antiquities," that " it signifies primarily a place or region, and, in combination with other words, a place of plenty or abundance; . . ." a name " most applicable to a region which is richer in the ' chief things of the ancient mountains, the precious things of the lasting hills, and the precious things of the earth and of the deep that coucheth beneath,' than any other portion of America of similar dimensions."

We naturally infer that the name is French; but our researches prove that it was originally the Indian *Aquoddie*, a pollock, — not a poetic or romantic significance. This was corrupted by the French into *Accadie, L'Acadie, Cadie.*

So little originality in nomenclature is shown in America, that we could desire that Indian names should be retained; that is, when not too long, or harsh in sound; yet in *this* case we are inclined to rejoice at the change from the aboriginal to the more musical modern title.

Though a vast extent of territory was once embraced under that name, it is now merely a rather fanciful title for a small part of the Province of Nova Scotia.

Acadia! The Bay of Fundy! There's magic even in the names; the very sound of them calling up visions of romance, and causing anticipations of amazing displays of Nature's wonders. Fundy! the marvel of our childhood, filling the mind's eye in those early school days with that astounding picture, — a glittering wall of green crystal, anywhere from ten to one hundred feet in height, advancing on the land like the march of a mighty phalanx, as if to overwhelm and carry all before it! Had it not been our dream for years to go there, and prove to our everlasting satisfaction whether childish credulity had been imposed upon?

Our proposed tourists, eight in number, being a company with a leaning towards music, bound to be harmonious, desiring to study the Diet-tonic as illustrated by the effects of country fare and air, consolidate under the title of the Octave. The chaperone, who we all know is a dear, is naturally called "Do"(e); one, being under age, is dubbed the Minor Third; while the exclamatory, irrepressible, and inexhaustible members from the Hub are known as "La" and "Si."

INTRODUCTION. 15

Having decided upon our objective point, the next thing is to find out how to reach it; and here, at the outset, we are surprised at the comparative ignorance shown regarding a region which, though seemingly distant, is in reality so accessible. We are soon inclined to quote from an old song,—

"Thou art so near and yet so far,"

as our blundering investigations seem more likely to prove how not to get anywhere!

But we set to work to accumulate railroad literature in the shape of maps, schedules, excursion books; and these friendly little pamphlets prove delightful pathfinders, convincing us how readily all tastes can be suited; as some wish to go by water, some by land, and some by "a little of both." Thus, those who are on good terms with old Neptune may take a pleasant voyage of twenty-six hours direct from Boston to the distant village of Annapolis, Nova Scotia, which is our prospective abiding place; while those who prefer can have "all rail route," or, if more variety is desired, may go by land to St. John, New Brunswick, and thence by steamboat across the Bay of Fundy. At last the company departs on its several ways, and in sections, that the dwellers in that remote old town of historic interest may not be struck breathless by such an invasion of foreigners.

The prime mover of the expedition, having already travelled as far east as Bangor, commences the journey at night from that city. Strange to say, no jar or unusual sensation is experienced when the iron horse passes the boundary; nor is anything novel seen when the train known as the "Flying Yankee" halts for a brief breathing spell at MacAdam Station. A drowsy voice volunteers the information: "It is a forsaken region here." Another of our travellers replies, "Appearances certainly indicate that the Colossus of *Roads* is absent, and it is to be hoped that he is mending his ways elsewhere." Then the speakers, tipping their reclining chairs to a more recumbent posture, drift off to the Land of Nod.

With morning comes examination of travellers' possessions at the custom-house, with amusing exhibitions of peculiarly packed boxes and bags, recalling funny episodes of foreign tours, while giving to this one a novel character; then the train speeds on for seven hours more.

THE BAY OF FUNDY.

OVER THE BORDER.

THE BAY OF FUNDY.

Ere long singular evidence of proximity to the wonderful tides of the Bay of Fundy is seen, as all the streams show sloping banks, stupendously muddy; mud reddish brown in color, smooth and oily looking, gashed with seams, and with a lazily moving rivulet in the bed of the stream from whence the retreating tide has sucked away the volume of water.

"What a Paradise for bare-footed boys, and children with a predilection for mud pies!" exclaims one of the tourists; while the other — the practical, prosaic — remarks, "It looks like the chocolate frosting of your cakes!" for which speech a shrivelling look is received.

This great arm of the sea, reaching up so far into the land, and which tried to convert Nova

Scotia into an island (as man proposes to make it, by channelling the isthmus), was known to early explorers as La Baie Françoise, its present cognomen being a corruption of the French, *Fond-de-la Baie.*

Being long, narrow, and running into the land like a tunnel, the tide rises higher and higher as it ascends into the upper and narrowest parts; thus in the eastern arm, the Basin of Minas, the tidal swell rises forty feet, sometimes fifty or more in spring.

In Chignecto Bay, which extends in a more northerly direction from the greater bay, the rise has been known to reach seventy feet in spring, though it is usually between fifty and sixty at other times. Here, in the estuary of the Petitcodiac, where the river meets the wave of the tide, the volumes contending cause the Great Bore, as it is called; and as in this region the swine wade out into the mud in search of shell fish, they are sometimes swept away and drowned. The Amazon River also has its Bore; the Indians, trying to imitate the sound of the roaring water, call it "pororoca."

In the Hoogly it is shown; and in a river of China, the Teintang, it advances up the stream at the rate of twenty-five miles an hour, causing a rise of thirty feet. In some northern countries the Bore is called the Eagre. Octavius says this must be because it screws its way so *eagrely* into the land, but is immediately suppressed, and informed that the name is a corruption of Oegir, the Scandinavian god of the sea, of whom we learn as follows: —

Odin, the father of the gods, creator of the world, possessing greatest power and wisdom, holds the position in Scandinavian mythology that Zeus does in the Greek. Like the Olympian Jupiter, he held the thunder-bolts in his hand; but differed from the more inert divinity of Greece in that, arrayed in robes of cloud, he rode through the universe on his marvellous steed, which had eight feet. This idea was characteristic of a hardy race living a wild outdoor life in a rigorous climate. Oegir, the god of the sea, was a jotun, but friendly to Odin. The jotuns were giants, and generally exerted their powers to the injury of man, but, not being gifted with full intelligence, could be conquered by men. The first jotun, named Ymer, Odin subdued, and of his flesh formed the earth, of his bones the mountains; the ocean was his blood, his brains the clouds, while from his skull the arch of the heavens was made.

We resolved to witness the singular spectacle of the Oegir of Fundy; but, not receiving answer to our application for accommodations at Moncton, proceeded on our way, consoling ourselves with the thought that we could see a bore any day, without taking any special pains or going much out of our way.

The Basin of Minas! What a "flood of thoughts" rise at the name. Fancy paints dreamy and fascinating pictures of the fruitful and verdant meadow land, the hills, the woods, the simple-hearted, childlike peasants; upright, faithful, devout, leading blameless lives of placid serenity:

"At peace with God and the world."

It seemed that there must be some means of crossing the beauteous Basin whence the broken-hearted exiles sailed away so sadly; and that any tourist with a particle of romance or sentiment in his composition would gladly make even a wide detour to visit it. Therefore we were surprised to learn that railroad schedules said nothing of this route, and that it seemed almost unknown to summer pleasure seekers. Not to be deterred, however, what better can one do than write direct for information to Parrsboro, — a pretty village, which is the nearest point to the Basin. Thus we learn that a short railway, connecting with the Intercolonial, will convey us thither, though not a road intended for passenger service.

"It will only add to the novelty and interest of our tour," we say. We rather hope it will prove a *very* peculiar road, and are prepared for discomfort which we do not find; although, at Spring Hill, the point of divergence from the main line, such a queer train is waiting, that one exclaims, "Surely we have come into the backwoods at last!"

The car is divided in the middle, the forward part devoted to baggage, while in the rear portion, on extremely low-backed and cushionless seats, beside tiny, shadeless windows, sit the passengers. And such passengers! We mentally ejaculate something about "Cruikshank's caricatures come to life." With much preliminary clanking of chains, a most dolorous groaning and creaking of the strange vehicle, a shudder and jar, the train is in motion, and slowly proceeding through densely wooded and wild country, — a coal and lumber district, where only an occasional log house relieves the monotony of the scene, — log huts which look as if they have strayed away from the far South and dropped down in this wilderness. At intervals, with a convulsive jerk which brings to their feet some new travellers on this peculiar line, the train halts to take on lumber; and one of our tourists remarks, "This old thing starts like an earthquake, and stops as if colliding with a stone wall;" and continues: "Do you think the poet who longed for 'a lodge in some vast wilderness,' would have been satisfied with this?" Without waiting for a reply, the next remark is: "We are looking for summer accommodations; don't you think we could find board cheap here?" The prosaic one, ignoring such an attempt at pleasantry, replies, "Five dollars per thousand feet, I have been told."

When the conductor, in a huge straw hat and rough suit, *sans* collar or cravat, comes to collect tickets, the satirical one asks, "Will he punch them with his penknife, or clip them with a pair of old scissors?"

We have

> "Heard of the wonderful one-hoss shay,
>   That was built in such a logical way
>   It ran a hundred years to a day,"

and conclude that the S. H. & P. R. R. resembles it somewhat; and that, although there is a "general flavor of mild decay" about it in some respects, it will not be in danger of wearing out from high rate of speed; but who cares about *time* when on a holiday?

At last, in the distance, a range of blue hills becomes visible, with a faint, far gleam of water; and, as the blue line abruptly descends to the glistening streak below, we know in an instant what that promontory must be, and ecstatically quote with one voice, —

"Away to the northward Blomidon rose,"

regardless of geography, as that Cape happens, in this case, to be south of us.

Having received information by mail that "hosses and carages" are to be found at Parrsboro, and that the sailing of the steamer is "rooled by the tide," eager looks are cast about on alighting at that charming village, the natives of which, to our surprise, are not backwoodsmen or rough countrymen. Mine host, genial and gentlemanly, becomes visible; and we are soon bowling merrily along through the neat village, the picturesque country beyond, and are set down at a refreshingly old-timey inn directly on the shore of the Basin of Minas, which bursts suddenly upon the view, amazing one by its extent and beauty. We exclaim in surprise, "Why, it looked no larger than one's thumb nail on the map!"

THE BASIN OF MINAS.

THE BASIN OF MINAS.

A CURVING beach with rolling surf, a long and very high pier, showing the great rise of the tide, — at this point sixty feet in the spring, — and directly before one the peculiarly striking promontory of Blomidon, with the red sandstone showing through the dark pines clothing his sides, and at his feet a powerful "rip" tossing the water into chopped seas; a current so strong that a six-knot breeze is necessary to carry a vessel through the passage which here opens into the Bay of Fundy.

This is the place where schedules said nothing of a boat to convey the tourist across the inland sea — of thirty miles' width — to the railroad on its south shore, — the line which bears on its rolling stock the ominous initials W. A. R., but passes through the most peaceful country nevertheless. Yet our genial host's assurances that such a vessel will come are not to be doubted; and, after a dainty repast, a group sits on the pier, watching ghostly ships and smaller craft emerge from and vanish into the mist. As the mists disperse and the moon comes out clearly, it reveals the " Hiawatha " approaching, — a graceful propeller of five hundred tons burden, and one hundred and some odd feet in length.

Partridge Island, which is close at hand, commands exceptionally fine views, as Blomidon does also; the famous Capes d'Or and Chignecto, seven hundred and thirty to eight hundred feet high, with Advocate Harbor, are within pleasant driving distance. There are twenty varieties of minerals on Blomidon; as many more, with jaw-testing names, on Partridge Island "and thereabout;" so in this locality a geologist would become quite ecstatic. Some of the finest marine scenery of the Provinces, as well as lovely inland views and the noted and singular Five Islands, can be seen within a radius of twenty miles.

" No country is of much interest until legends

and poetry have draped it in hues that mere nature cannot produce," says a pleasant modern writer.

Geologists believe that the range of hills known as the North Mountain was once a long narrow island, and that a shoal gradually formed near Blomidon, in time filling in until that headland became part of the mainland.

This striking cape, five hundred and seventy feet high, one would naturally expect to find associated with strange wild myths of the aborigines; and

> "Ye who love a nation's legends,
> That like voices from afar off
> Call to us to pause and listen,"

attend then!

It seems that this was the favorite resort of Glooscap, the Indian giant, who, like "Kwasind the Strong Man," in "Hiawatha," entered into a fierce combat here with the Great Beaver (Ahmeek, King of the Beavers, is spoken of in that same poem), and contended with the gigantic creature in similar manner, throwing huge masses of rock, which, falling in the water, became, in this case, the Five Islands. The Indian legend says that at this point a stupendous dam was built by the Great Beaver; and because this was flooding the Cornwallis valley, Glooscap, whose supernatural power was unlimited, broke and bent it into its present shape, forming Cape Blomidon, afterwards strewing the promontory with gems, some of which he carried away to adorn "his mysterious female companion." Here also he held a wonderful feast with another giant; and, ordinary fish not sufficing to satisfy their enormous appetites, the two embarked in a stone canoe, sailed out into the Great Lake of Uniras, as they called the Basin, and there speared a whale, which they brought to the shore and devoured at short notice. The approach of the white man causing the Indian giant to desert his old haunts, he sailed out on the great water and vanished from sight; but some day, when men and animals live together in peace and friendship, he will return and resume his royal sway on the Basin of Minas. Before his departure he gave a farewell feast to all the

OLD FRIENDS' ALMSHOUSE.

animals, who swarmed from all over the country, turned his dogs into stone, and left his kettle overturned in the shape of an island near Cape Spencer, across Minas Channel. Since that time the loons, who were his hunters, wander sadly about the wildest lakes and rivers, searching for their master, uttering their dolorous cries; and the owls keep up their part of the lament, crying "Koo koo skoos," which, being Indian language, they evidently learned from the giant, and, being interpreted, signifieth "I am sorry."

The crown of France is adorned with a fine amethyst from Blomidon; and those early explorers, De Monts and Co., "found in the neighborhood" (of Parrsboro) "chrystals and blue stones of a shining colour, similar in appearance to those known by the name of Turkeese." One of the company, "having found a beautiful specimen of this kind, broke it into two pieces, and gave one to De Monts, and the other to Poutrincourt, who, on their return to Paris, had them handsomely set by a jeweller, and presented them to the King and Queen."

At the base of Cape d'Or there is a very powerful current with great maelstroms; this is known as the Styx, and through these terrible whirlpools two fishermen were carried this season (1883), one losing his life; while the other, an expert swimmer and athlete, was saved by less than a hair's-breadth, and afterwards described most thrillingly his sensations on being drawn into and ejected from the frightful vortices.

Just at daybreak, when Blomidon looks out all glowing from the gauzy veil of mist, as the lazy zephyr wafts it aside, and the placid water repeats the glorious tints of radiant clouds, we regretfully take our departure. Cape Sharp and Cape Split, bold promontories which stand like mighty sentinels guarding the entrance to the Bay of Fundy, appear in clearest azure and violet; while the mountains of the north shore are sharply defined in pure indigo against the brilliant sky, as the propeller steams away. The sail across, two hours and a half in length, is a vision of ideal and poetic beauty, all too brief; and as we step ashore we feel tempted to quote, "Take, oh boatman, thrice thy fee!"

At this point (Hantsport) we take the W. and A. R. R., and in a few hours are set down at the place which we have been so long planning to reach; the place of which our host, who is probably not familiar with the history of St. Augustine, Florida, wrote proudly as "the oldest town in North America."

It certainly is one of the oldest settlements in North America, having been founded in 1604, and, until 1750, it was the capital of the whole peninsula of Nova Scotia: Annapolis, — the old Port Royal, the historical town which has been the scene of so many struggles and bitter contentions; but is now the very picture of peace and utterly restful quiet.

Here the Eight settle down for a long sojourn; basking in the delicious atmosphere, devoting themselves to searching out the most picturesque views, in a series of rambles, drives, and excursions, and visiting all points for miles around, to which history and romance have added charms almost as great as those of river and mountain which they always possessed.

Those of our party who hail from the city of Brotherly Love naturally feel a special interest in Acadia and the sad story of Longfellow's heroine; as a patent for the principality of Acadia, which included the whole American coast from Philadelphia to Montreal, was given by the "impulsive and warmhearted monarch," Henry IV. of France, to Pierre du Guast, the Sieur de Monts, constituting him governor of that country, and giving him the trade and revenues of the region.

Consequently some of the ancestors of our Philadelphia friends were Acadians, though not French peasantry.

There also : —

"In that delightful land which is washed by the Delaware's
   waters,
 Guarding in sylvan shades the name of Penn the apostle,
 Stands on the banks of its beautiful stream the city he
   founded.
 There all the air is balm, and the peach is the emblem of
   beauty,

And the streets still re-echo the names of the trees of the
 forest,
As if they fain would appease the Dryads whose haunts
 they molested.
There from the troubled sea had Evangeline landed, an exile,
Finding among the children of Penn a home and a country."

In that sedate and sober city was

" the almshouse, home of the homeless.
Then in the suburbs it stood, in the midst of meadows
 and woodlands;
Now the city surrounds it; but still, with its gateway and
 wicket
Meek in the midst of splendor, its humble walls seem to
 echo
Softly the words of the Lord, — 'The poor ye have always
 with you.' "

There the sad exile's weary search was at last rewarded; the long-parted lovers were reunited, though but for a moment on the verge of the grave; and thus was ended

" the hope and the fear and the sorrow,
All the aching of heart, the restless, unsatisfied longing,
All the dull, deep pain, and constant anguish of patience!"

The city almshouse stood, we are told, at the corner of Twelfth and Spruce Streets; but the belief is quite general (and we incline decidedly to that) that our beloved poet intended by his description to portray the quaint building formerly known as the Friends' Almshouse, which stood in Walnut Place (opening off of Walnut Street below Fourth), and which was torn down in 1872 or 1873 to give place to railroad and lawyers' offices.

The entrance from the street, by "gateway and wicket," as the poem says, led through a narrow passage way; and there faced one a small, low-roofed house, built of alternate red and black bricks (the latter glazed), almost entirely covered by an aged ivy which clambered over the roof. The straggling branches even nodded above the wide chimneys; at both sides of the door stood comfortable settles, inviting to rest; and the pretty garden charmed with its bloom and fragrance. The whole formed such a restful retreat, such an oasis of quiet in the very heart of the busy city, that one was tempted often to make excuses for straying into the peaceful enclosure.

In a book printed for private circulation in Philadelphia some years ago, there is an item of interest about the Acadians. The author narrates that she and a young companion, in their strolls to the suburbs, where they went to visit the Pennsylvania Hospital (Eighth and Pine Streets, now in the heart of the city), were timid because obliged to pass the place where the "French Neutrals" were located.

These people, because they were foreigners, and there was some mystery about them which the girls did not then understand, inspired them with fear; though Philadelphia residents of that time testify that the homeless and destitute strangers were in reality a very simple and inoffensive company, when, "friendless, homeless, hopeless, they wandered from city to city." Through the influence of Anthony Benezet, a member of the Society of Friends, they were provided with homes on Pine Street above Sixth, where the two little wooden houses still stand; one, when we last saw it, being painted blue.

What a picturesque company of adventurers were those French noblemen, who, turning their backs upon the luxuries and fascinations of court life, sailed away to this wild and distant land, where, in the pursuit of gain, fame, or merely adventure, they were to suffer absolute privation and hardship; consorting with savages in place of the plumed and pampered denizens of palaces.

After a probably tempestuous voyage across the bleak Atlantic, and a merciless buffeting from Fundy in the spring of 1604, the prospective Governor of the great territory known as Acadia was sailing along this coast, which presents such a forbidding aspect from the Bay, making his first haven May 16. At that time, we can readily imagine, in this northern region the weather would not be very balmy. Even now the wild rocky shore stretches along drearily — though with certain stern picturesqueness — as far as eye can reach, and then must have been even less attractive, as it showed no sign of habitation.

Champlain was somewhat familiar with these shores from former voyages, and so had been chosen as pilot; but De Poutrincourt and Pontgravé, other associates of Pierre du Guast, the

Sieur de Monts, doubtless looked askance at each other, or indulged in the expressive French shrug as the cheerless panorama passed before them. On that 16th of May, at the harbor where the little town of Liverpool is now situated, De Monts found another Frenchman engaged in hunting and fishing, ignoring, or regardless of, the rights of any one else; and without ado this interloper (so considered by De Monts) was nabbed; the only consolation he received being the honor of transmitting his name, Rossignol, to the harbor, — a name since transferred to a lake in the vicinity.

After a sojourn of two weeks at another point (St. Mary's Bay), the explorers proceeded northward; and at last a particularly inviting harbor presented itself, causing the mental vision of the new Governor and his company to assume more hopeful aspect, as they turned their course thither and pronounced it " Port Royal!"

PORT ROYAL.

PORT ROYAL.

HERE they managed to exist through the winter with as much comfort as circumstances would admit of; but with the return of summer were on the wing again, in search of more salubrious climate and more southerly locality for the establishment of a colony, sailing along the coast of Maine and Massachusetts as far as Cape Cod.

Attempts were made to establish settlements, but the natives proved unfriendly; the foreigners had not a sufficient force to subdue them; and, as De Monts was obliged to return to France, De Poutrincourt and his companions established themselves again at Port Royal. Here, to while away the long winter, the gay adventurers established a burlesque court, which they christened "L'Ordre de Bon Temps;" and of the merry realm each of the fifteen principal persons of the colony became supreme ruler in turn. As the Grand Master's sway lasted but a day, each one, as he assumed that august position, prided himself on doing his utmost to eclipse his predecessor in lavish provision for feasting. Forests were scoured for game; fish were brought from the tempest-tossed waters of the Bay, or speared through the ice of L'Équille; so the table fairly groaned with the luxuries of these winter revellers in the wilds of Acadia. With ludicrous caricature of court ceremonial, the rulers of the feast marched to the table, where their invited guests, the Indian chiefs, sat with them around the board; the squaws and children squatting on the floor, watching for bits which the lively company now and then tossed to them. "They say" that an aged sachem, when dying, asked if he should have pies in heaven as good as those which he had eaten at Poutrincourt's table!

To the Indians, the greatest delicacy of all on the table was bread. This, to them a dainty viand, they were always ready to consume with gusto; but were invariably averse to grinding the corn, although promised half of the meal as recompense for their labor. The grinding was performed with a hand-mill, and consequently so laborious and tedious that the savages would rather suffer hunger than submit to such drudgery, which they also seemed to think degrading to the free sons of the forest.

Proverbially fickle are princes; and of this De Monts was convinced on his return to France, for during his absence he had lost favor with his sovereign, Henry IV., who revoked his commission; still he succeeded, after many difficulties, in procuring supplies for his colony, and arrived just in time to prevent his people from leaving Port Royal discouraged and disheartened. One member of the little community of Frenchmen was Lescarbot, a lawyer, who was talented, poetical, and did much to enliven the others during the absence of their leader, who, on his return, was received by a procession of masqueraders, headed by Neptune and tritons, reciting verses written by Lescarbot. Over the entrances to the fort and to the Governor's apartments were suspended wreaths of laurel and garlands surrounding Latin mottoes, — all the work of the pastimist (if one may coin such a word). The relief and encouragement brought by De Monts were but temporary, and in the spring (1606) news was received that nothing more could be sent to the colonists, and they must be disbanded.

Imagination portrays the strange picture presented at this time in this remote region: the gay French courtiers vanishing from the sight of their Indian comrades almost as suddenly and mysteriously as they had appeared but three years before, and leaving their dusky boon companions lamenting on the shore. The eyes of the savages — that race who pride themselves on their stoicism — were actually dimmed with tears as they watched the vessel fading away in the distance.

For four years "ye gentle sauvage" pursued the even tenor of his way, and consoled himself as best he could for the absence of the lively revellers who had cheered his solitude; then, presumably to his delight (in 1610), he saw Poutrincourt returning. That nobleman had

promised the king to exert himself for the conversion of the Indians. Three years later a company of Jesuits sailed for this port with the same object in view; but, losing their reckoning, they founded settlements at Mt. Desert instead.

Madame de Guercheville, a true woman indeed, who was honored and respected in a dissolute court where honor was almost unknown, had become a zealous advocate of the conversion of Indians in America; and through her means and influence several priests of the Jesuit order were sent out in 1612 to this settlement. The sachems, with members of their tribes living at Port Royal, were baptized, twenty-one at one time, with much show of rejoicing typified by firing of cannon, waving of banners, blaring of trumpets. Some doubt is expressed whether the savages fully understood what it was all about, and what their confession of faith fully signified; as one chief, on being instructed in the Lord's Prayer, objected to asking for bread alone, saying that he wished for moose flesh and fish also; and when one of the priests deliberately set to work, with notebook and quill, to learn the language of the aborigines by asking one man the Indian words for various French ones (to him totally incomprehensible), the savage, with malice aforethought, purposely gave him words of evil signification, which did not assist the Frenchman in enlightening other members of this benighted race. Perceiving the trick which had been played upon him by the savage, who had been so perplexed by his questioning, the priest declared that Indian possessed by the Devil! However, with all its discouragements, this was the opening of the work of the Jesuits in America; in which even those who might have thought their zeal at times mistaken could not but respect them for the noble heroism, displayed during so many years, in their work of civilizing and enlightening the savages.

Even in these olden times there were turbulent marauders abroad; and one such, Argall, from Virginia, after destroying the settlement at Somes Sound (Mt. Desert), pounced upon this peaceful station, destroying the fort and scattering the colonists (1613).

The section known as Virginia was granted in 1606 to the London and Plymouth Companies; and as that portion embraced the country between 34° and 45° north latitude, it seems that Argall pretended that the French at Port Royal were interlopers, usurping his rights; but as De Monts had received in 1604 a charter for the country defined as lying between 40° and 46° north latitude, Argall had no right to dispossess De Monts or his successor.

Notwithstanding that a member of Argall's company speaks of him as "a gentleman of noble courage," that does not prevent us from considering him a rascal; for at this time France and England were at peace, and he was unauthorized in his base and tyrannous invasion of Port Royal. Before his attack on this quiet, peaceful station, he had shown greatest treachery at Somes Sound, Mt. Desert, where he stole Saussaye's commission and cast adrift in an open boat fifteen of the colonists.

Poutrincourt's son, Biencourt, was now Governor of Acadia, and stationed at Port Royal. He endeavored to make terms with Argall, and offered to divide with him the proceeds of the fur trade and the mines; but this was refused, and the settlement broken up, some of the unfortunate Frenchmen joining Champlain at Quebec, some scattering into the woods among the Indians, while others were carried to England and from thence demanded by the French ambassador. Thus, after only a little more than eight years from the time of settlement, the colony was entirely broken up.

En passant: A friend of ours, who with his family passed a summer in New Hampshire, "at the roots of the White Mountains," as some one expressed it, surprised an old farmer by asking the names of hills in sight from that particular locality. The reply was, "I dono, and I dono as I *care;* but you city folks, when you come here, are allers askin' questions." We conclude that we are liable to be classed in a similar category; and, in fact, the Dabbler when sketching one day is asked, "Ain't some of your party writing a book?" The interrogator's mind is set at rest by being answered that the reason we have become animated notes of interrogation is because we are interested in the history of the old town; but it is fearful to think for what that innocent lad is responsible: putting notions in people's heads, and causing this volume to be inflicted on a suffering world!

To return to our subject. The olive branch was not yet to be the emblem of this spot, now so peaceful, for a colony of Scotch people were next routed (1628), and the place left in ruins, when a season of quiet ensued; but this was virtually the commencement of the French and English wars in North America, continuing, with slight intermissions, until the treaty of 1763, by which France gave up her possessions in America.

In 1634 Port Royal fell into French hands again, when Claude de Razilly was Governor, and here for a short time lived La Tour, one of his lieutenants, who kept up such bitter feuds with D'Aulnay, who held like position to his own, and whose story Whittier relates in his poem, "St. John, 1647."

Madame de la Tour must have been one of

the earliest advocates of women's rights, as she so bravely held the fort of St. John in her husband's absence.

> "'But what of my lady?'
> Cried Charles of Estienne.
> 'On the shot-crumbled turret
> Thy lady was seen:
> Half veiled in the smoke-cloud
> Her hand grasped thy pennon,
> While her dark tresses swayed
> In the hot breath of cannon!
>
> Of its sturdy defenders,
> Thy lady alone
> Saw the cross-blazoned banner
> Float over St. John.
>
> Alas for thy lady!
> No service from thee
> Is needed by her
> Whom the Lord hath set free:
> Nine days, in stern silence,
> Her thraldom she bore,
> But the tenth morning came
> And Death opened her door!'"

Hannay says she was "the first and greatest of Acadian heroines, — a woman whose name is as proudly enshrined in the history of this land as that of any sceptred queen in European story."

For a long series of years this post of Port Royal was the bone of contention between the French and English; the fort, being held for a time by one power, then by the other, representing the shuttle-cock when these contending nations battled at her doors. In 1654 the place was held by the French under Le Borgne. An attack by the English was successful, though the French were well garrisoned and provisioned.

In De Razilly's time La Tour, who might have been satisfied with his possessions at St. John, assailed it; then English pirates took the fishing fleet (1684); next Sir William Phipps captured and pillaged the fort in 1690. Shortly after this, pirates from the West Indies plundered the place; and in 1691 it again fell into the hands of the French under De Villebon. It was still to undergo two sieges in 1707, when, under Subercase, the besiegers were repulsed; and in 1710 seven ships with English marines bombarded the fort for several days. The garrison at last, being in starving condition, were forced to yield; and the victors christened the place Annapolis Royal, in honor of their sovereign then reigning in Great Britain.

The subjugation of this part of "New France" made Nova Scotia an English province; and for a time this realm might have answered to the description of Rasselas's Happy Valley; the thrifty, honest people relieved from "wars and rumors of wars," and taking up the quiet, contented routine of every-day life.

> "Far from the madding crowd's ignoble strife
> They kept the noiseless tenor of their way."

But in 1744 the reign of siege and terror began again, and the town was destroyed by bombardment and incendiary fires, when, for nearly three months, Laloutre and Duvivier besieged the fort. The garrison, augmented by troops from Louisburg, and assisted by provisions and men from Boston, finally repulsed their assailants. The next year there was another assault under De Ramezay, which was unsuccessful; and after the dispersion of the Acadians (1755), the much-fought-over place was allowed to remain in quiet until 1781, when two American ships-of-war sailed up the river at night. Their forces, taking the fort by surprise, robbed the houses, after imprisoning the people in the old block-house. Since that time the English have retained possession of this much-disputed territory; the fort has been unarmed and unoccupied (by military force) since 1850, when the Rifle Brigade were stationed here; but the tedium of garrison life proving still more irksome here, and desertions being frequent, the fort was abandoned as a military post.

ANNAPOLIS.

ANNAPOLIS.

What a fascination there is about that old fort at Annapolis! — "the hornet's nest," as it was called in the olden time; the stronghold which withstood so many sieges, and was the subject of constant contentions in by-gone years.

The hours slip by unnoted when one sits on the ramparts dreaming and gazing on the broad sweep of river, the distant islands, the undulating lines of the mountain ranges. The sleepy-looking cows wander lazily about, cropping the grass on the embankments, and even clamber over the ancient archway.

One peoples the place with imaginary martial figures, and is almost startled when the stillness is broken by a rustle and approaching footsteps, and turns, as if expecting to see glittering uniforms appearing through the crumbling arch; but it is only old Moolly, who deliberately walks into the inner enclosure, and, if "our special artist on the spot" has left his sketch for a moment, probably puts her foot in it, with the air of one who should say, "Who are you who dare invade my realm?"

The quaint barrack building, with its huge chimneys and gambrel roof, is now occupied by several families; and a whitewashed fence encloses a gay garden. The small magazine, built of creamy sandstone sent from France for the purpose, still remains, and its excessively sharp roof shows above the ramparts; but the massive oaken door stands open wide and is green with age; the roof is decidedly shaky; and the shingles hang loosely, so that one would think that only a moderate gale would send them flying like a pack of cards.

The block-house, built of massive logs and heavy planks of English oak, stood within the past year by the bridge over the moat; but, unfortunately, a person without reverence for antiquities has razed it, thereby obtaining his winter fuel cheaply; and he now turns an honest penny by selling canes, etc., of the wood.

When we indignantly ask some of the townspeople how they could have permitted this, they reply, "Oh, it was getting rotten, and would have tumbled down some day;" but we judge, by pieces which we see of the sound, tough-fibred oak, that it might have stood for fifty years more without injury; while a little judicious propping and repairing, perhaps, would have preserved it for a longer period than that. Poor Annapolitans, who had no Centennial Exhibition to teach them the value of historical relics and "old things"!

On the Maine Central Railroad, quite near the track at Winslow, we passed, on our way here, an old block-house, which is carefully preserved.

Not long ago, the Canadian Government received orders that all buildings, except the barrack and magazine, must be removed from the fort enclosure; yet a garrulous old Scotchman still resides there in a tiny house, and plies his trade as cobbler.

His delight is to regale strangers with preposterous "yarns," and accounts of his adventures in her Majesty's service; accounts which must be taken with considerably more than the proverbial grain of salt, but to which we listened with delight and amazingly sober countenances. When asked how it happens that he still remains in the fort grounds, he answers, " I writ out home, to Angland, to say that I serrved in the arrumy fur thurty yeer, and I know the ould gurrul will let me stay." (There's respect for a sovereign!)

He talks wisely of the "bumpruf," a word which we have some difficulty in translating into *bomb proof;* and we are, apparently, overpowered with wonder as he explains how " with a few berrls av pouther they cud send ivery thing flying, and desthroy the whole place, avery bit av it."

Presumably misled by our simulated credulity, he goes on to describe a well in front of the magazine, and says, " When they wanted to get red av throoblesome preesoners, ploomp they'd go in the watter, and thet was the last

av 'em!" Suffice it to say, that the oldest inhabitant has no recollection of the slightest trace of such a well.

The underground passage has fallen in; only the entrance being now visible and accessible. Old Gill says, "I was the last man iver in it; and I got caught there with the wall fallin' in, and they were twinty fower hours gettin' me out;" (a li[c]kely story!) adding, "Oh, I was a divil in them days!" and "I found in there a bit av a goon wrinch" (gun wrench); and Mr. So and So, from Halifax, "gev me some money fur it, an' he lapped it up in his han'kerchef like as if it had ben goold."

We are told of an ancient house "of the era of the French occupation," and go to see it; but learn, though it looks so aged, that it was built upon the *site* of the French house, and is not the old original. The owner has reached the ripe age of ninety-four, and is a remarkable man, with the polished manner of a gentleman of the old school. In such a climate as this, one would naturally expect to find centenarians. He tells us many interesting things about old times here, and his grandson brings out a barrel of Acadian relics to show us.

We are interested in noting the differences between these ancient implements and those in use at the present time; here is a gridiron, with very long handle and four feet (a clumsy quadruped), and we see in fancy the picture of home comfort, as the busy housewife prepares the noonday meal, where —

"Firmly builded with rafters of oak, the house of the farmer
Stood on the side of a hill commanding the sea, and a shady
Sycamore grew by the door, with a woodbine wreathing around it."

Here, too, are ox chains, a curiously shaped ploughshare, an odd little spade used in mending the dikes and digging clay for bricks, and also the long and heavy tongs of the "blacksmith," —

"Who was a mighty man in the village and honored of all men:
For since the birth of time, throughout all ages and nations
Has the craft of the smith been held in repute by the people."

These implements were discovered at Frenchman's Brook on this farm, only three years ago, and were when found apparently as bright and strong as if just placed there. They were covered with brush, but a foot or two below the surface; and seem to have been hurriedly hidden by the exiles, who, finding them too weighty for conveyance, secreted them, probably with the hope of returning sometime.

What a study for an artist the group would have made, as they stood examining the rusty iron, and talking of the unhappy people so ruthlessly sent into banishment! For background, the quaint, unpainted house, black with age, the roof of the "lean-to" so steeply sloping that the eave-trough was on a line with the heads of the group. Beyond lay the lovely valley, with the winding Équille on its serpentine way to join the greater river; the whole picture framed in the long range of wooded and rugged hills.

Higginson thinks there has been too much sentimentalizing over the fate of the Acadians; and one member of our party so evidently considers that our enthusiasm savors of the gushing school-girl, that we are cautious in our remarks. But the old man's grandson, holding his pretty child on his shoulder, and looking across the valley to his pleasant dwelling, says, "Oh, it was cruel to send them away from their homes!" to which all earnestly assent.

Clambering up the hill back of the old house, we come upon the site of an ancient French church, and commend the taste of those who chose such an admirable location. Here we find, to our delight, that local tradition has buried two fine old bells. Bells! What a charm there is about them! One of the earliest recollections of our childhood is of a bell, which, being harsh and dissonant, so worked upon our youthful sensibilities as to cause paroxysms of tears; and now in these later years we are sure that should some genie set us down blindfolded in any place where we had ever remained for a time the mere tones of the bells would enlighten us as to our whereabouts.

> "Those evening bells! Those evening bells!
> How many a tale their music tells,
> Of youth and home and that sweet time
> When last I heard their soothing chime."

After the Port Royal settlement was broken up by Argall in 1613, tradition says this church crumbled away into ruin, and, as the supporting beams decayed, the bells sank to the ground, where, from their own weight and the accumulations of Nature's *débris*, they became more and more deeply embedded until lost to view. Silver bells, from France, they say. Of course! Who ever heard of any ancient bells which were not largely composed of that metal? It is a pretty myth, however, which we adopt with pleasure; though common sense plainly says that silver would soon wear away in such use; that the noble patrons of a struggling colony in a wild country would not have been so extravagant as that; and that bell metal is a composition of copper and tin which has been in use from the time of Henry III.

The people of Antwerp have special affection for the "Carolus" of their famous cathedral; and that bell is actually composed of copper, silver, and gold; but it is now so much worn that they are not allowed the privilege of hearing it more than once or twice a year. "Kings and nobles have stood beside these famous caldrons" (of the bell founders), "and looked with reverence on the making of these old bells; nay, they have brought gold and silver, and pronouncing the holy name of some saint or apostle which the bell was hereafter to bear, they have flung in precious metals, rings, bracelets, and even bullion."

Possibly these old bells of Annapolis, the secret of whose hiding-place Nature guards so well, were made by Van den Gheyn or Hemony of Belgium, who from 1620 to 1650 were such famous founders that those of their works still extant are worth their weight in gold, or priceless, and are noted the world over for their wonderful melody. If so, when they

"Sprinkled with sounds the air, as the priest with his hyssop
Sprinkles the congregation and scatters blessing among them,"

it was no doubt with silvery tone; and, as it is well known that bells sound best when rung on a slope or in a valley where there is a lake or river, doubtless this wide and lovely stream carried the music of the mellow peal, and returning voyagers heard the welcome notes; as the sailors of the North Sea, on entering the Scheldt, strain their ears to catch the faint, far melody of the chimes of the belfry of Antwerp, visible one hundred and fifty miles away.

Another day we make an expedition to see the Apostle Spoons, and are received, as invariably everywhere, with cordial hospitality. These spoons would, I fear, cause the eye of an antiquary to gleam covetously. They have round, flat bowls about two and a half inches in diameter; narrow, slender, and straight handles, terminating, the one with a small turbaned head, the other with a full-length figure about one inch long; the entire length of the handles being about four and a half inches.

In the bowl of one the letters P L I are rudely cut; and on both is stamped something which, they say, under magnifying glass resembles a King's head. In the spring of 1874 or 1875 these were turned up by the plough, in a field two miles beyond the town, the discovery being made in the neighborhood of the supposed site of an old French church. The farmer's thrifty housewife was making soap at the time the spoons were unearthed; and as they were much discolored, "the old lead things" were tossed into the kettle of lye, from whence, to her amazement, they came out gold, or, at least, silver washed with gold. These spoons, they say, were used in the service of the church; but it is more likely that they were the property of some family, and probable that they were dropped by their owners — then living beyond the present site of Annapolis — when, at the time of the banishment of the Acadians, they were hurried away to the ships on the Basin of Minas.

An apostle spoon was often a treasured heirloom in families of the better class, and at the advent of each scion of the family tree was suspended about the neck of the infant at baptism, being supposed to exert some beneficent influence.

Especially in the East, about the seventh century, we find that a small vessel, or spoon, sometimes of gold, was used in the churches. These were eucharistic utensils, by means of which communicants conveyed the sacred elements to the mouth; but this custom was forbidden and done away with, though probably the tradition of such usage suggested the spoon, which became general in Greek and most Oriental churches many years after. The supposition is, that in those churches, after the wafer had been put into the wine in the chalice, the spoon was used to dip out such portion as was to be reserved for administering the last sacrament to the dying, or to those who were too ill to attend the service in the church. In all churches of the East, except the Armenian, the spoon is used in administering the sacrament.

Curious customs also existed in ancient times in reference to baptism. Honey mixed with milk or with wine was given to the one who had just received this rite, to show that he who received it, being a newly born child spiritually, must not be fed with strong meat, but with milk. This became a regular part of the ritual, and was closely adhered to. The old customs of festivals of rejoicing, public thanksgivings, wearing of garlands, singing of hymns, and giving presents, are well known and familiarly associated with baptismal festivities.

The presentation of apostle spoons at christenings was a very ancient custom in England. A wealthy sponsor or relative who could afford it, gave a complete set of twelve, each with the figure of an apostle carved or chased on the end of the handle; while sometimes a poor person presented only one, but on that was the figure of the saint for whom the child was named. Sometimes this rudely moulded little figure represented the patron saint of the sponsor or the donor. In 1666 the custom was on the decline.

An anecdote relating to this usage is told of Shakspeare. The latter "stood godfather" to the child of a friend; and after the ceremonies of the christening, as the poet seemed much absorbed and serious, the father questioned him as to the cause of his melancholy.

The sponsor replied, that he was considering what would be the most suitable gift for him to present to his god-child, and that he had finally decided. "I'll give him," said he, "a dozen good latten spoons, and thou shalt translate them." This was a play upon the word Latin. In the Middle Ages a kind of bronze used for church and household utensils was known as "latten;" and the same name was applied in Shakspeare's time to thin iron plate coated with tin, of which domestic utensils and implements were made.

In Johnson's "Bartholomew Fair" one of his characters says, "And all this for the hope of a couple of apostle spoons, and a cup to eat caudle in." In a work of Middleton, entitled "The Chaste Maid of Cheapside," one of the characters inquires, "What has he given her?" to which another replies, "A faire high standing cup, and two great 'postle spoons, one of them gilt."

The hat, or flat covering on the head of the figure, — that which we call a turban in one of these at Annapolis, — was a customary appendage and usual in apostle spoons; the intention being thereby to protect the features of the tiny heads from wear. Whatever the history of these at Annapolis, there can be no doubt of their genuineness, and, in a perfect state, they are extremely rare.

In our antiquarian researches we are naturally drawn to the old cemetery, adjoining the fort grounds; but learn that the oldest graves were marked by oaken slabs, which have all disappeared, as have also many odd stone ones. But among those still standing one records that some one "dyed 1729;" another states that the body below "is deposited here until the last trump;" and one, which must be the veritable original of the "affliction sore" rhyme, ends: "till death did sieze and God did please to ease me of my pain." Still another bears this epitaph, *verbatim et literatim:* —

"Stay friend stay nor let thy hart prophane
The hu^mble Stone that tells you life is vain.
Here lyes a youth in mouldring ruin lost
A blofsom nipt by death's untimely frost.
O then prepare to meet with him above
In realms of everlasting love."

The stone-cutter's hand must have been as weary when he blundered over the word humble as the poet's brain evidently was when he reached the line which limps so lamely to the conclusion. Near this recently stood a stone,

"With uncouth rhymes and shapeless sculpture decked,"

on which the representation of Father Time was carved in such peculiar manner that from pose and expression the figure might have passed for a lively youth rather than the dread reaper, and was irreverently known to the village youths as "Sarah's young man," a title suggested by a popular song of the day.

In a remote corner we find the tomb of "Gregoria Remonia Antonia," "a native of Spain;" and afterwards learn her story, — an episode in the life of the Iron Duke which does not do him honor. Did *la grande dame*, the Duchess, ever know of the fair foreigner who supplanted her, the dame o' high degree, in her husband's affection? Did the beautiful Spanish maiden dream, when the brilliant English General wooed her, that he was doing her and another woman the greatest wrong? Little did the fascinating Spaniard think that the so-called "nobleman" would compel her to marry another; and that other a rough, illiterate man, who would bring her to this wild, strange, far-away country, and that here she should be laid to rest "after life's fitful fever." Is it to be wondered at that her fiery Southern spirit rebelled, that her wrongs embittered her, and that her life here was unhappy?

To add to the romance, one who attended her in her last illness tells us that when the garrison gave a ball, the slender little Spanish lady loaned or gave "pretty fixins" to the young girls to wear, and appeared herself in rich silks and plumes; that she gave to her attendant in that illness a wonderful box "all done off with, — well — this here plated stuff, you know;" and that when the end was drawing near, the faint, weak voice, with its broken English (at best so difficult to understand), tried to make "Char-loet-tah" comprehend where she must look for something hidden away which she wished her nurse to have in recognition of her services. But alas! the hoarded treasure was not found until months after the poor soul was gone, and then fell into the very hands which the sad alien had most desired should not touch it.

The old adage about a sailor's right to have "a sweetheart in every port" is still cited in these days of boasted advancement in culture, religion, morals; and it is the same old world to-day as that which lauded and bowed down to him whom it called "his Grace" (despite what we consider his grace-less actions); the same world, alas! ignoring the open and evident fact when he steps aside from the narrow path of honor and rectitude; while, should she swerve in the least, pouring out mercilessly its harshest taunts, or overwhelming her with pitiless scorn. This, because woman should hold an exalted position, and "be above suspicion"? Then why do not the so-called "lords of creation," as they might and ought, set an example of noble uprightness to "the weaker vessel," guiding, guarding, upholding her through "the shards and thorns of existence"?

The Spanish girl, left an orphan by the wars in which the dashing and gallant English officer figured so proudly, fell to the care of two aunts, who, belonging to that indolent, pleasure-loving race of sunny Spain, perhaps left the poor girl too much to her own devices, and thus she may have been more easily beguiled.

"Look here, upon this picture, and on *this :* " first, the gay little señorita, holding daintily in her tapering fingers a cigarette, which she occasionally raises to her " ripe red lips," afterwards languidly following with her lustrous black eyes the blue wreaths of smoke as they float above her head and vanish in the air; next, the withered crone, with silver hair, wrinkled skin, and no trace of her early beauty, sitting in the chimney corner, and still smoking, though now it is a clay pipe, — to the amazement and disgust of the villagers. Yet we, believing in the only correct interpretation of *noblesse oblige*, and that he only is truly noble who acts nobly, have only pity for the poor soul who here laid down life's weary burden twenty-two years ago at the age of seventy-two, and scorn for him who rests in an honored grave, and is idealized among the world's heroes.

How amusing it is to hear the people speak of us invariably as "Americans," as if we were from some far-away and foreign country, and to hear them talk of England as "home"!

The hearty cordiality, natural manner, and pleasantly unworldly ways of the people are most refreshing; in "a world of hollow shams," to find persons who are so *genuine* is delightful; and thus another charm is added to give greater zest to our enjoyment.

One, half in jest, asks a Halifax gentleman how they would like to be annexed to the United States, and is quite surprised at his ready and earnest reply: "Annexed? Oh, yes, we'd be glad to be; . . . we would n't come with empty hands; we have what you want, — fisheries, lumber, minerals; we'd not come as paupers and mendicants. . . . It will come, though it may not be in our day. . . . The United States would not wish to purchase, — she has done enough of that: we would have to come of our own free will; and we would, too!"

Then there is the elderly Scotch gentleman, who appropriately hails from the place with the outlandish name of Musquodoboit. He tells us that during the "airly pairt" of his residence in America he visited in the States, and that he has seen "fower Preesidents" inaugurated.

Of his first attendance at such a ceremony he says: "An' whan I see thet mon, in hes plain blek coat, coomin' out amang all o' thim people, an' all the deeguetirries in their blek coats tu, an' not a uniforrum amoong thim, I said, 'This is the coontry fur me,' — it suited my taste. An' how deeferint it wud be in Yerrup, where there wud be tin thausind mooskits aboot, to kep 'im from bein' shot."

On our way here we were told: "Oh, you'll find Annapolis hot!" It might perhaps seem so to a Newfoundlander; but to us the climate is a daily source of remark, of wonder and delight. It is balmy, yet bracing; and though there may be times when at midday it is decidedly warm, — as summer should be, — the nights are always cool, and we live in flannel costumes and luxuriate.

ANNAPOLIS.

Warner speaks of "these northeastern lands which the Gulf Stream pets and tempers;" yet he passed through this dear old town without stopping, remarking only that he could not be content for a week here, and felt no interest in the place apart from its historic associations. Let him stop next time and investigate. We flatter ourselves that we could enlighten him somewhat.

Our friends at various shore and mountain resorts report constant fogs; yet we can testify that in nearly seven weeks' residence here there were but two mornings which were foggy, and on those days the gray screen was rolled away at noon.

"aloft on the mountains
Sea-fogs pitched their tents, and mists from the mighty Atlantic
Looked on the happy valley, but ne'er from their station descended."

That singular feature spoken of in Longfellow's poem is shown here: the mists rise from the Bay and rest lovingly, caressingly, on the crests of the long range of mountains, giving them the appearance of comfortable warmth under this downy coverlet on cool nights; but this fleece very rarely descends to the valley.

Dr. O. W. Holmes must have had such a place as this in mind when he said: —

> " And silence like a poultice came
> To heal the blows of sound ; "

and surely tympanums most bruised by the world's clangor and jar could not fail here to be soothed and healed; and the writer of " Oh, where shall rest be found?" would have received answer to his query here also. The quiet is astonishing: there are no farm sounds even; and, though the hours pass so pleasantly that we "take no note of time," we can tell when Saturday comes, for then numbers of log-laden ox-carts plod slowly into the village from the back country.

The bells on the animals' necks tinkle precisely like the sound of ice when carried in a pitcher of water; and consequently do not jar upon one's ear in this quietude as the clanking herd-bells which we hear in some farming regions of the States.

At night the only break in the profound stillness is when the tide is ebbing, and the Équille can be heard rushing under the bridge a quarter of a mile away. We cannot discover the meaning of that word, and so consult a foreign relative, who tells us that at Dinard, in France, they catch the *équille*, — a small fish, also called a *lançon*, because it darts in and out of the sand, and in its movements is something like an eel.

That certainly describes this peculiar stream, for surely it would be difficult to find one with a more circuitous course. It forms two horseshoes and an ox-bow connected, as we see it from our windows; and when the tide is out diminishes to a rivulet about two feet in width. At flood it is more than twice the width of the Wissahickon, and when the high tides of August come its magnitude is surprising.

Then we understand why the hay-ricks (which we wickedly tell our friends from the "Hub" resemble gigantic loaves of Boston brown bread) are on stilts; for, regardless of dikes or boundaries, this tortuous creek spreads over its whole valley, as if in emulation of the greater river of which it is a tributary. Haliburton says that for a time this was called Allan's River, and the greater one was named the Dauphin; but we are glad that the old French name was restored to the serpentine creek, as it is so much better suited to its peculiar character.

The great event of the week is the arrival of the Boston steamer, when all the town turns out and wends its way to the wharves.

The peculiar rise of the tide (thirty feet) is here plainly shown, as one week the passengers step off from the very roof of the saloon, and next time she comes in they disembark from the lowest gangway possible and climb the long ascent of slippery planks to the level above.

The river shows curious currents and counter-currents, as bits of *débris* are hurrying upward in the middle of the stream, while similar flotsam and jetsam rush away as rapidly down stream along both shores.

The queer old tub of a ferry-boat, with its triangular wings spreading at the sides, — used as guards and " gang planks," — is a curiosity, as it zigzags across the powerful current to the village on the opposite shore.

But " the ferryman's slim, the ferryman's young, and he's just a soft twang in the turn of his tongue;" and in our frequent trips across he probably makes a mental note when he hears us lamenting that we cannot get lobsters, for one day he sends to our abiding place four fine large ones, and will not receive a cent in remuneration.

Another time, when waiting for the farmer's son to guide us to the " ice mine," — a ravine in the mountains where ice remains through the summer, — a delicious lunch, consisting of fresh bread, sweet milk, and cake, is unexpectedly set before us, and the generous farmer's wife will not listen to recompense.

A modern writer says: "A great part of the enjoyment of life is in the knowledge that there are people living in a worse place than that you inhabit;" but it does not add to our happiness to think of those who could not come to this lovely spot; and we commiserate the Can't-get-away Club of the cities.

We would not change places with any of the dwellers at the fashionable resorts at springs, sea, or mountains, — no, indeed! though they no doubt would elevate their noses, and set this place down at once as "deadly dull," or "two awfully slow for anything!"

Doubtless those also of our friends to whom we tell the plain, unvarnished truth, if they come here will be disappointed, as they will not see with our eyes. One cannot expect the luxuries of palatial hotels at five dollars per day; such would be out of place here.

At our abiding place, which looks like a gentleman's residence, and is, as one of the Halifax guests says, "not a bit like an 'otel," there is an extensive garden, from which we are regaled with choice fresh vegetables daily; and we have *such* home-made butter! (The bill of fare "to be issued in our next"). A Frenchman might think that "we return to our muttons" frequently; still, as that viand suggests at least the famous English Southdown in excellence, we are resigned.

A noted wit has said: "Doubtless God might

have made a better berry than the strawberry, but doubtless God never did;" and if one is so fortunate as to come to this country in proper season he can feast on that delectable fruit in its perfection, — that is, the wild fruit, so much more delicious and delicate in flavor than after its boasted "improvement" by cultivation. If one arrives before the close of the fisheries, salmon, fit for a royal banquet, graces the table; while even in July and August he may enjoy shad; and strange enough it seems to Philadelphians to be eating that fish at such time of year.

There are in the town a number of inns, and summer guests are also made welcome and comfortable in many of the private residences. In one of the latter — a large old-fashioned house, with antique furniture — three sisters reside, who possess the quiet dignity and manner of the old school; and here one would feel as if visiting at one's grandfather's, and be made pleasantly "at home."

We are surprised to find that this old town has generally such modern and New-Englandish aspect; and are told that it has twice been nearly destroyed by fire, even in modern times; therefore but few of the quaint buildings remain. Some of these are picturesque and interesting, the one combining jail and court-house being a feature of the main street. The window of one of the cells faces the street; and the prisoner's friends sit on the steps without, whiling away the tedium of incarceration with their converse.

The oldest dwelling in the town stands on St. George's Street, nearly opposite the old-fashioned inn known as the Foster House. Its walls were originally made of mud from the flats, held together by the wiry marsh grass, which, being dried, was mixed in the sticky substance as hair is in plaster; but as these walls gave way from the effects of time the seams and cracks were plastered up, and by degrees boarded over, until now the original shows only in one part of the interior.

The houses throughout this region are almost invariably without blinds or outside shutters, and consequently look oddly to us, who are inclined to screen ourselves too much from "the blessed sunshine." Bay windows are popular.

We saw one small house with four double and two single ones, giving it an air of impertinent curiosity, as the dwellers therein could look out from every possible direction. The ancient dormer windows on the roofs have given place to these queer bulging ones, which, in Halifax especially, are set three in a row on the gray shingles, and bear ludicrous resemblance to gigantic bee-hives.

In some of the shops, at the post-office and railroad station, our money is taken at a small discount; but in many of the shops they allow us full value for it. In one the proprietor tells us of the sensation caused here once by the failure of a Canadian bank, and the surprise of the town's-people — whose faith seemed shaken in all such institutions — when he continued to take United States bank-bills. He says: "I told 'em the United States Government had n't failed, that I believed in it yet, would take all their money I could get, and be glad to have it, too!"

To continue the impression of being in a foreign land; we must attend service at the five or six different churches, and hear the prayers for the Queen and Royal Family. In the first place of worship, where the Octavo augments the congregation, Victoria and many of her family are mentioned by full name and title, in sonorous and measured tones; in the next the pastor speaks of "Our Sovereign, and those under her and over us;" in another "Our Queen" is simply referred to; and some ministers who are suspected of being tinctured with republicanism sometimes forget to make any special allusion to her Majesty.

In our walks up the main street, which is not remarkably bustling or busy, we see long rows of great old hawthorn bushes bordering the road, and giving quite an English touch to the scene; and everywhere gigantic apple-trees, which would delight an artist, so deliciously gnarled and crooked are they.

I am not aware that astronomy is a favorite study with the inhabitants, but have no doubt that *cidereal* observations are popular at certain seasons, — as this country is a famous apple-growing district, and that fruit is sent from here to England and the States in vast quantities. Octavius says, "If you would know what ann-apol-is, you should come here in the fall," but is at once frowned down by the other seven for this atrocity.

The valleys of Annapolis and Cornwallis yield an average crop of two hundred thousand barrels of apples. Dealers in Bangor who paid $7 per barrel in Boston for this fruit, have afterwards been chagrined on discovering that it came from Annapolis originally, and that they could have procured the same from that place direct at $2.25 to $3 per barrel.

Very lovely is the view from a hill outside the village, and there also is the Wishing Rock, — one of the most noted objects of interest, as a guide-book would term it. "They say" that if one can run to the top without assistance, or touching the rock with the hands, then whatever one wishes will "come true." This feat it is almost impossible to accomplish, as the stone has been worn smooth by countless feet before ours; still the youthful and frisky members of our party must attempt the ascent, with a run, a rush, and a shout, while the elders look on, smiling benignly.

The dikes of L'Équille form a peculiar but pleasant promenade; and along that narrow, circuitous path we frequently wander at sunset. These embankments remain, in great part, as originally built by the Acadians, and are formed of rubbish, brush, and river mud, over which sods are closely packed, and for most of the season they are covered with tall waving grass. This primitive sea-wall is six or eight feet in width at the base, and only about one foot wide at the top, so it is necessary for him "who standeth" to "take heed lest he fall;" otherwise his enthusiasm over the beauties of the prospect may receive a damper from a sudden plunge into the water below.

There is a fine new rink in the village; and in the mornings those of us who are novices in the use of rollers have a quiet opportunity to practise and disport ourselves with the grace of — a bureau, or other clumsy piece of furniture on wheels!

Then we go to the wharves to witness the

lading of lumber vessels. Some of the logs floating in the water are so huge as to attest that there are vast and aged forests somewhere in her Majesty's domains in America; and the lumbermen, attired in rough corduroy, red shirts, and big boots, balance themselves skilfully on some of the slippery trunks, while with pole and boat-hook propelling other great ones to the gaping mouths in the bow of the vessel. Then horse, rope, pulley, and windlass are brought into play to draw the log into the hold and place it properly among other monarchs of the forest, thus ignominiously laid low, and become what "Mantalini" would style "a damp, moist, unpleasant lot." From the wharf above we look down into the hold, and, seeing this black, slimy, muddy cargo, say regretfully, "How are the mighty fallen!" as we think of the grand forests of which these trees were once the pride and glory, but of which ruthless man is so rapidly despoiling poor Mother Earth.

We have brought with us those aids to indolence which a tiny friend of ours calls "hang-ups," expecting to swing them in the woods and inhale the odors of pine; but the woods are too far away; so we are fain to sit under a small group of those trees at the end of the garden and gaze upon the peaceful valley.

"There in the tranquil evenings of summer, when brightly
  the sunset
Lighteth the village street, and gildeth the vanes on the
  chimneys,"

we sit, when

"Day with its burden and heat has departed, and twilight
  descending
Brings back the evening star to the sky, and the herds to
  the homestead."

There we sit and talk of the romantic story, comparing notes as to our ideal of the heroine; and such is the influence of the air of sentiment and poetry pervading this region, that we decide that Boughton's representation of her,

"When in the harvest heat she bore to the reapers at noon-
  tide
Flagons of home-brewed ale, . . .
Nut-brown ale, that was famed for its strength in the village of Grand Pré,"

is too sturdy, as with masculine stride she marches a-field; and that Constant Meyer's ideal more nearly approaches ours. The one depicts her in rather Puritanic attire; the other, studying authentic costume, they say, shows her

"Wearing her Norman cap, and her kirtle of blue, and the
  ear-rings,
Brought in the olden time from France, and since, as an
  heirloom
Handed down from mother to child, through long genera-
  tions;"

and seated by the roadside, as,

"with God's benediction upon her,
. . . a celestial brightness — a more ethereal beauty —
Shone on her face and encircled her form."

All along the roads we notice a delicate white blossom, resembling the English primrose in shape, and one day ask an intelligent-looking girl whom we meet what it is called; she does not know the name, but says the seed was accidentally brought from England many years ago, and the plant "has since become quite a pest," — which we can hardly understand as we enjoy its grace and beauty. We notice that our pleasant informant follows a pretty fashion of other belles of the village, — a fashion which suits their clear complexions and bright faces; that is, wearing a gauzy white scarf around the hat, and in the dainty folds a cluster of fresh garden flowers.

The artist Boughton says: "The impressionist is a good antidote against the illusionist, who sees too much, and then adds to it a lot that he does not see." If he had ever visited this place we wonder what his idea would be of this quaint poem, supposed to have been written in 1720, which we have unearthed.

We have acquired quite an affection for this pleasant old town, and shall be loath to leave. If our friends think we are too enthusiastic, we shall refer them to this old writer to prove that we have not said all that we might; as he indulges in such airy flights of fancy and such extravagant praise.

His description would lead one to expect to see a river as great as the Mississippi, and mountains resembling the Alps in height, whereas in reality it is a quiet and not extraordinary though most pleasing landscape which here "delights the eye."

ANNAPOLIS-ROYAL.

The King of Rivers, folemn calm and flow,
Flows tow'rd the Sea yet fcarce is feen to flow;
On each fair Bank, the verdant Lands are feen,
In gayeft Cloathing of perpetual Green;
On ev'ry Side, the Profpect brings to Sight
The Fields, the Flow'rs, and ev'ry frefh Delight:
His lovely Banks, moft beauteoufly are grac'd
With Nature's fweet variety of Tafte.
Herbs, Fruits and Grafs, with intermingled Trees
The Profpect lengthen, and the Joys increafe:
The lofty Mountains rife to ev'ry View,
Creation's Glory, and its Beauty too.
To higher Grounds, the raptur'd View extends,
Whilft in the Cloud-top'd Cliffs the Landfcape ends.
Fair Scenes! to which fhould Angels turn their Sight;
Angels might ftand aftonifh'd with Delight.
Majeftic Groves in ev'ry View arife
And greet with Wonder the Beholders' Eyes.
In gentle Windings where this River glides,
And Herbage thick its Current almoft hides;
Where fweet Meanders lead his pleafant Courfe,
Where Trees and Plants and Fruits themfelves difclofe;
Where never-fading Groves of fragrant Fir
And beauteous Pine perfume the ambient Air;

The air, at once, both Health and Fragrance yields,
Like fweet Arabian or Elyfian Fields.
Thou Royal Settlement! he wafhes Thee;
Thou Village, bleft of Heav'n and dear to me:
Nam'd from a pious Sov'reign, now at Reft,
The laft of Stuart's Line, of Queens the beft.

 Amidft the rural Joys, the Town is feen,
Enclof'd with Woods and Hills, forever green:
The Streets, the Buildings, Gardens, all concert
To pleafe the Eye, to gratify the Heart.
But none of thefe fo pleafing or fo fair,
As thofe bright Maidens, who inhabit there.

 Your potent Charms fair Nymphs, my verfe infpire,
Your Charms fupply the chafte poetic Fire.
Could thefe my Strains, but live, when I 'm no more,
On future Fame's bright wings, your names fhould foar.

 Where this romantic Village lifts her Head,
Betwixt the Royal Port and humble Mead;
The decent Manfions, deck'd with mod'rate coft,
Of honeft Thrift, and gen'rous Owners boaft;
Their Skill and Induftry their Sons employ,
In works of Peace, Integrity and Joy.
Their Lives in Social, harmlefs Blifs, they fpend,
Then to the Grave, in honor'd Age defcend.
The hoary Sire and aged Matron fee
Their profp'rous Offfpring to the fourth Degree:
With Grief fincere, the blooming offfpring clofe
Their Parent's Eyes, and pay their Debt of Woes;
Then hafte to honeft, joyous Marriage Bands,
A newborn Race is rear'd by careful Hands:
Thro' num'rous Ages thus they 'll happy move
In active Bufnefs, and in chafteft Love.

ANNAPOLIS.

The Nymphs and Swains appear in Streets and Bowers
As morning freſh, as lovely as the Flowers.
As bright as Phoebus, Ruler of the Day,
Prudent as Pallas, and as Flora gay.

A Spire majeſtic rears its ſolemn Vane,
Where Praiſes, Pray'r and true Devotion reign;
Where Truth and Peace and Charity abound,
Where God is ſought, and heav'nly Bleſſings found.
The gen'rous Flock reward their Paſtor's care,
His Pray'rs, his Wants, his Happineſs they ſhare.
Retir'd from worldly Care, from Noiſe and Strife,
In ſacred Thoughts and Deeds, he ſpends his Life;
To mo'drate Bounds, his Wiſhes he confines,
All views of Grandeur, Pow'r and Wealth reſigns;
With Pomp and Pride can chearfully difpenſe
Dead to the World, and empty Joys of Senſe,

The Symphony of heav'nly Song he hears,
Celeſtial Concord vibrates on his Ears,
Which emulates the Muſic of the Spheres.
The Band of active Youths and Virgins fair,
Rank'd in due Order, by their Teacher's Care,
The Sight of all Beholders gratify,
Sweet to the Soul, and pleaſing to the Eye.
But when their Voices found in Songs of Praiſe,
When they to God's high Throne their Anthems raiſe,
By theſe harmonious Sounds ſuch Rapture 's giv'n,
Their loud Hoſannas waft the Soul to Heav'n:
The fourfold Parts in one bright Center meet,
To form the bleſſed Harmony complete.
Lov'd by the Good, eſteemed by the Wiſe,
To gracious Heav'n, a pleaſing ſacrifice.

> Each Note, each Part, each Voice, each Word confpire
> T' inflame all pious Hearts with holy Fire;
> Each one in Fancy feems among the Throng
> Of Angels, chanting Heav'n's eternal Song.
>   Hail Mufic, Foretafte of celeftial Joy!
> That always fatiafts, yet canft never cloy:
> Each pure, refin'd, extatic Pleafure's thine,
> Thou rapt'rous Science! Harmony divine!
>   May each kind With of ev'ry virtuous Heart
> Be giv'n to all, who teach, or learn thine Art:
> May all the Wife, and all the Good unite,
> With all the Habitants of Life and Light,
> To treat the Sons of Mufic with Refpect,
> Their Progrefs to encourage and protect.
> May each Mufician, and Mufician's Friend
> Attain to Hymns divine, which never end."

Being a musical company, the Octave accept this peroration without criticism, and do not seem to consider it an extravagant rhapsody, though they are so daring as to take exception to other parts of the queer old poem.

As we have come here for rest, we are not disturbed at finding that trains, etc., are not always strictly "on time." We are summoned at 7.15 A.M., but breakfast is not served for more than an hour after; we engage a carriage for two o'clock, and perhaps in the neighborhood of three see it driving up in a leisurely manner. The people are wise, and do not wear themselves out with unnecessary rush and hurry, as we do in the States. The train advertised to start for Halifax at 2 P.M. more frequently leaves at 3, or 3.30; but then it has to wait the arrival of the steamboat which, four times per week, comes across from St. John. The express train requires six hours to traverse the miles intervening between this quiet village and that not much livelier town, while for the accommodation train they allow ten hours; but when one comes to see beautiful country one does not wish to have the breath taken away by travelling at break-neck speed.

We know that some of our party are capable of raising a breeze, and we are on a gal(e)a time anyhow; still, this is a remarkably breezy place, the wind rising with the tide, so we understand why there are so few flowers in the gardens, — the poor blossoms would soon be torn to pieces; but the windows of the houses generally are crowded with thriving plants gay with bloom, giving most cheery effect as one strolls about the town.

In our excursion to the Bay Shore we halt to water the horses at a neat little cottage on the summit of the North Mountain, and even here the little garden (protected from the winds by a fence) is all aflame with a wonderful variety of large double and gorgeous poppies. From this point, also, we have our first view of the wide Bay, shimmering in the hazy sunlight far below, and can faintly trace the rugged hills of New Brunswick in the distance.

Rapidly descending, we follow the coast for several miles, finally stopping at a lonely house on the rocky and barren shore, — such a wild spot as a novelist would choose to represent a smuggler's retreat; but the family would not answer his purpose in that respect, for they are homely and hospitable, agreeing at once to provide stabling for our horses and to sell us some milk for our lunch. They drop their net-mending, come out *en masse*, and, on learning that some of us are from Philadelphia, greet us like old friends, because their eldest daughter is living in that distant city. The best pitcher is brought out for our use, the whole establishment placed at our disposal, and, finding that we will be so insane as to prefer to picnic under the few straggling pines by the water instead of using their dining-room, several march ahead to show the way to the rocky point; and we form a long and, of course, imposing procession.

As we gaze along this barren and lonely shore, Octavia exclaims, "Imagine the amazement of De Monts when he sailed along this iron-bound coast and suddenly came upon that wonderful gateway which leads into the beautiful Annapolis Basin and the fertile, lovely region beyond!" and we all agree that it is a shame that the embouchure should now be known by the vulgar title, Digby Gut, instead of its old cognomen, St. George's Channel. "Why couldn't they call it the Gap or the Gate?" one exclaims; "that wouldn't be quite so dreadful."

One evening some of our pleasant acquaintances in the town come to take us to Lake La

Rose, away up on the South Mountain; and there we embark and glide over the placid water in the moonlight, rousing the echoes with song, and vainly endeavoring to uproot the coy lilies, which abruptly slip through our fingers, and "bob" down under the water as if enjoying our discomfiture. But as Dame Nature tries her hand at painting in water-colors, treating us to a series of dissolving views, the shower forces us to hurry back to the village again.

Before leaving this "vale of rest," we must see the widely extended panorama from the Mackenzie road, where hills beyond hills stretch away to the horizon, and the lovely valley spreads itself like a map below. The bird's-eye view from Parker's Mountain must also be seen, and many other excursions accomplished. The old cannon of Lower Granville also is "one of the sights." This ancient piece of ordnance was fired in old times to notify the quiet country folk when news was received from England. At such times relays, seven to ten miles apart, mounted in hot haste and carried the messages on until Digby was reached; and from thence a vessel conveyed the news to Boston.

As we are talking of all we have seen in this region, and of our various enjoyments, Octavia exclaims, "Some persons thought we could not be content here for a week; yet more than six have slipped away, and I'm sure I don't want to go! I shall tell my friends that though we are 'remote,' the rest of the quotation does not apply, for we are neither 'unfriended,' 'melancholy,' nor 'slow!'"

How often has it been our fate, when among the mountains of New Hampshire, to see the grand ranges disappearing behind a thick curtain of smoke, which, daily growing denser, at last almost completely blots out Nature's pictures, so there is no use in undertaking excursions for the sake of fine views. The explanation is invariably "fires in the Canada woods;" and here, in this "cool, sequestered vale," we have an opportunity of seeing forest fires before we take our departure for other fields of observation. After sunset we are apparently almost surrounded by volcanoes, as the lurid flames leap up into the deepening blackness of the night; and when we lovers of Nature, distressed afterwards by seeing vast tracts all scarred and desolate, exclaim, "Why did n't they stop it? Why did they allow it?" echo answers, "Why?"

One day we learn that a mill on L'Équille is threatened, and expect that there will be some excitement; but a very old-fashioned fire-engine, with clumsy hand-power pumps, goes lumbering by, followed by men and boys, who walk in a leisurely and composed manner. The mill is saved by some means, however; and we rejoice, as it is, so to speak, historical, standing in a place favored for such purposes since Lescarbot's time; even Argall (in 1613), when demolishing other buildings of the village, having spared the mill which occupied the site of the present one.

In our various wanderings we visit the Indian settlement at the head of this crooked stream, but find its residents too civilized to be very picturesque. We are interested in learning what the Canadian Government does for their welfare, and wish a similar policy could be instituted in the States. Here, as with us, liquor is their curse. The once famous chief of the Micmacs lives at Bear River, and is addicted to the bottle. One day a young girl, who was a summer guest at this place, sat down on an overturned canoe which this chief (now known as James Meuse) had just completed; and, as the bark bent with her weight, the wily Indian pretended that the boat was irretrievably ruined. The girl's father, asking what amount would compensate for the damage, received reply, " Ten, twenty, dollar ; " and receiving thirty dollars from the generous stranger, Redskin remarked afterwards that he " wished more girl come sit on boat," and probably turned the money into liquid fire, and poured it down his throat in a short space of time. As there is a heavy fine for selling liquor to Indians, one of that race will never divulge from whom he has received it, however intoxicated he may be.

Another Indian sachem noted in history — Membertou — lived to the age of one hundred and four, and was buried at Annapolis, then Port Royal, with military honors, as befitted the companion of soldiers. At Poutrincourt's table he was a daily and honored guest in that olden time, and, when the "Order of Happy Times" was instituted there, of course became a *member too!* Query: Did that ancient convivial society offer suggestions to the famous old "State in Schuylkill Club" of Philadelphia when they were organizing so many years after?

DIGBY.

DIGBY.

In the drive to Digby, twenty-one miles, we pass along all the ins and outs of the shore of Annapolis Basin, finding the succession of views on that curiously land-locked harbor a perfect study and delight, and more picturesque than on the trip to the same place by steamer, as we discover later.

There we see a bright-eyed, pretty little maiden, who wears a gay red handkerchief in place of a hat, and makes a picture as she drives her cow over a bit of moorland. Driver says she is "one of the French people," and that her name is Thibaudia, which, with its English signification (a kind of heath), seems appropriate for one living in the wilds, and deliciously foreign and suggestive. We wonder if old Crumplehorn understands French, and conclude that she is a well-educated animal, as she seems to obey directions without needing a touch of willow-branch to punctuate them.

> Sometimes it seems that the names conferred
> On mortals at baptism in this queer world
> Seem given for naught but to spite 'em.
> Mr. Long is short, Mr. Short is tall,
> And who so meek as Mr. Maul?
> Mr. Lamb's fierce temper is very well known,
> Mr. Hope plods about with sigh and groan, —
> "And so proceed ad infinitum."

At one point on our route, when we are passing through a lonely and apparently uninhabited region, our jolly driver, "Manyul," remarks, "Here's where Nobody lives;" and one replies, "Yes, evidently; and I should n't think any one would wish to." But a turn of the road brings a house in sight; and driver says, "That's his house, and his name is actually Nobody" (Charles, I believe). We quote, "What's in a name?" and conclude that if he is at all like the kindly people of this region whom we have met he may be well content to be nobody, rather than resemble many whom the world considers "somebodies," but who are not models in any respect.

Our driver is quite a character in his way, and in the winter he "goes a loggin'." On learning this we ply him with questions in such manner as would surprise a lawyer, eliciting in return graphic pictures of camp-life in New Brunswick wildernesses, and the amusements with which they while away the long evenings in their rough barracks. He describes their primitive modes of cooking, their beds of fragrant spruce boughs overlaid with straw, — "Better 'n any o' your spring mattresses, I tell *you!*" — the queer box-like bunks along the wall where they "stow themselves away," and where the most active and useful man is, for the time at least, literally laid on the shelf.

Octavius, thinking how much he would enjoy "roughing it" thus, asks what they would charge to take a young man to board in camp; and driver indignantly replies, "*Nothin'!* Do you suppose we'd charge board? No, *indeed!* Just let him come; and if we did n't give him a good time, and if he did n't get strong and hearty, then we'd be ashamed of ourselves and *sell out.*"

Here we approach a cove which driver calls

the Joggin (as it makes a cut or jog-in, we presume); and beyond, a wide arm of the Basin is spanned by a rickety old bridge, at least a quarter of a mile long, named in honor of her Majesty, — hardly a compliment to that sovereign, we think. The boards are apparently laid down without nails, and rattle like a fusillade as our vehicle rolls over them. Here and there planks are broken or gone entirely, showing the green swirling water beneath. Our chaperone, having more faith in her own feet than those of the horses, dismounts and walks across; while we, being naturally reckless and romantic, are willing to risk our necks for the sake of the charming views.

The village of Digby stretches along the shore, and from the hills surrounding it the Basin with its islands, the Gap, and Annapolis River, are charming.

Disciples of old "Izaak" would be likely to meet with greater success here than at Annapolis; as the current of the river at the latter place is so strong that, as a general thing, only the "old salts" are anglers; and they being most of the time out in the Bay or off on cruises, it follows that fish are scarce in the market.

An "ancient and fish-like smell" pervades the atmosphere in some parts of the village where the herring — humorously known as "Digby Chickens"— are spread on racks to dry; but this odor, the odd little shops and restaurants, the clumsy and queer lumber-boats, the groups of tars gossiping about doorways and wharves, only add to the nautical character of the place, and suggest reminiscences of "Peggoty," "Ham," and others of Dickens's characters.

We ignore the pleasant embowered hotel "in bosky dell," far up the street this time, though we visit it in a later sojourn; and, "just for the fun of it," take lunch in one of the peculiar little restaurants; where, seated at a minute table in one of the tiny calico-curtained alcoves, we partake of our frugal repast (the bill of fare is extremely limited), amusing ourselves watching the odd customers who come to make purchases at the counter across the room, and "making believe" that we are characters in an old English story.

On the bluff beyond the village, beneath great old Balm of Gilead trees whose foliage is perpetually in a flutter from the breeze through the Gap, there are several cannon, which it seems could not possibly have any hostile intent, but appear to be gratifying a mild curiosity by peering across the Basin and up the river beyond.

The long and very high pier stretches far out into the Basin, and upon it picturesque groups unconsciously pose for us, adding to the effect of the picture.

That the climate is salubrious and conducive to longevity we are convinced after visiting the cemetery, where one tomb records the demise of a man at the age of one hundred and two!

A peculiar taste for wandering among the tombs we have acquired in this summer jaunt. Here we see the tomb of one recorded proudly as "descended from the noble families of Stuart and Bruce," who, tradition says, was supposed to have held the position of servant to said scions of nobility. One who was known as a scoffer during life here is virtuously represented as "a sincere worshipper of Eternal, Almighty and ever just God;" reminding us of the popular adage, "lying like an epitaph." Twice have we seen one stone made to do service for two in an amusing manner: on the upper part the usual, "Sacred to the memory of," etc.; then half-way down had been carved a hand pointing to one side, and under it the words "There lies;" while the name, age, etc., of the later decedent was inscribed below the first.

One old tomb we were with this epitaph: —

> "Tho' gready worm destroy my skin
> And gnaw my wasting flesh
> When God doth build my bones agen
> He'll cloath them all afresh."

and another: —

> "What says the silent dead
> He bids me bear my load
> With silent steps proceed
> And follow him to God."

We notice that the English rule of the road maintains here, and our driver turns to the left when other vehicles are approaching. Captain C., who is from the States, tells us that he did not know of this custom, and in his first drive nearly collided with another vehicle, the driver of which thereupon used strong language. On being informed that he had almost overturned the conveyance of the Governor of Prince Edward's Island, the rash Yankee, undismayed, remarked, "Well, I don't care who he is, he don't know how to drive!"

HALIFAX.

HALIFAX.

Of course, as we are in the neighborhood, we must see the locality to which — in mild and humorous profanity — States people are sometimes assigned; and therefore proceed to Halifax and thoroughly "do" that sedate, quiet, and delightfully old-fashioned city.

En route, as the train passes beyond Windsor, one says, "Here we are out of sight of land;" and we then understand that it must have been some one from this locality who christened the valley of Annapolis the Garden of Nova Scotia; for here a scene of utter sterility and desolation meets the view: not a foot of earth is to be seen, but rocks are piled in wild confusion everywhere. A few dead trees stand among the *débris*, emphasizing the loneliness; and Conductor says when the world was created the "leavings" were deposited in this dreary tract.

By special arrangement with "Old Prob," there are none of the prevailing fogs during our stay; and Aurora Borealis gets up a special illumination. Regiments of red-coats, with torches and band, — aware doubtless of the presence of such distinguished strangers, — march past our hotel in the evening.

Though we are quartered in what is called the best hotel, it is a musty, fusty, rusty old building; and we agree with our friends among the residents (who vie with each other in showing us true English hospitality) who say they need an enterprising Yankee to start a good new hostelry, and "to show 'em how to run it."

Just at this time of year the city is full of summer tourists, many of whom come direct from Baltimore by the ocean steamships, which touch at this port; but, as we are subject to *mal-de-mer's* tortures, we rejoice that we came by "overland route."

Though our friends have engaged rooms for us beforehand, we are fortunate in securing apartments on the fourth floor, where peculiar coils of rope by the windows at once attract our attention. These, on examination, we find have big wooden beads (like the floats of a seine) strung on them at regular intervals; and this peculiar arrangement is a primitive fire-escape, which we are positive that no creature but a monkey could use with safety.

The prevailing fogs, and the use of soft coal, cause the buildings to appear dingy and rusty; but we like them all the better for that, as the city has a more foreign air, and, in some parts, quite strongly suggests Glasgow.

In the Parliament building we study the old portraits, concluding that the wigs must have been uncomfortable. Octavius wickedly hints that there *is* a fashion among ladies of the present time!—but as he does not tread on our toes, we ignore this insinuation, and turn our attention to the elaborate ornamentation of the wood-work—which is all antique hand-carving—in the council chambers; and are much interested in some rare old books in the Library,—among them a copy of the Psalms, three hundred years old; and another, with music, dated 1612. Here also we see and are actually allowed to handle a book, —

"PRESENTED
TO
THE LEGISLATIVE LIBRARY
OF
NOVA SCOTIA
IN MEMORY OF HER GREAT AND GOOD HUSBAND
BY
HIS BROKEN-HEARTED WIDOW
VICTORIA R"

and of course are duly overpowered at beholding the valuable autograph of that sovereign.

In one of the churches we are informed that a certain balustrade "is from America, and is all *marvel*," but do not find it marvellously beautiful nevertheless.

Of the gardens the natives are justly proud, as in this moist atmosphere plants, trees, and flowers flourish remarkably; still, we are not willing to concede that they are "the finest in America," as we have been told.

We conclude, as we pass the large Admiralty House, with its spacious and beautiful grounds, that Sir Somebody Something must find it a comfortable thing to be

"monarch of the sea, the ruler of the Queen's navee,"

and may with reason say, —

"When at anchor here I ride, my bosom swells with pride,"

while Halifax herself, with her famous harbor, in which the navy of a great and powerful nation could find safe anchorage, with room to spare, might justly finish out his song with the appropriate words concluding the verse: —

"And I snap my fingers at a foeman's taunts!"

Then the Citadel, the very name of which revives reminiscences of Quebec, and suggests something out of the every-day order of summer jaunts. As we ascend the hill to the fortress, the first thing attracting our attention is amusing. The "squatty" looking clock-tower, which appears as if part of a church spire, had been carried away by a high wind and dropped down on this embankment. Octavius says, "What a jolly place for coasting, if it were not for the liability of being plunged into the harbor at the foot!" as we mount the hill. At the gate we are consigned to the care of a tall soldier, whose round fatigue cap must be *glued* to his head, or it certainly would fall off, so extreme is the angle at which it inclines over his ear. A company of soldiers are drilling within the enclosure, their scarlet coats quite dazzling in the bright sunlight and in contrast with the cold gray granite; while others, at opposite angles of the walls, are practising signals with flags, the manoeuvres of the latter being quite entertaining as they wave the banners, now slowly, now rapidly, diagonally, vertically, horizontally, or frantically overhead, as if suddenly distraught. Probably this exercise could be seen in any of our forts; but as we are now beyond the borders of the United States, every detail interests us, and we have become astonishingly observant. The gloomy and massive bomb-proof walls of the soldiers' quarters appear quite prison-like, with their narrow windows; and our guide, speaking of the monotony of garrison life, rejoices that in a few months his

term of service will expire, and then he "will go to the States."

"The States" seem to be a Land of Promise to many people of this region; and, though this is gratifying to our national pride, we cannot but see that many make a mistake in going to "America;" as, for instance, the young girls of Annapolis, who, leaving comfortable homes, hie away to Boston, where, if they can get positions in an already crowded field, they wear themselves out in factories; or, having a false pride which prevents them from acknowledging failure and returning home, they remain until, broken down by discouragement and disappointment, compelled to accept charity. On this account the service at Annapolis is not what might be desired; and Octavius humorously wonders, when the "green hand" persistently offers him viands from the wrong side, "how he is expected to reach the plate unless he puts his arm around her."

"But we digress." As our party, with other sight-seers who have joined the procession, promenade about the fort, a culprit in the guard-room catches sight of the visitors as they pass, and, evidently for their hearing, sings mischievously, —

> "Farewell, my own!
>   Light of my life, farewell!
> For crime unknown
>   I go to a dungeon cell."

We conclude, as he is so musical about it, that he does not feel very much disgraced or oppressed by his imprisonment, though some one curiously inquiring "why he is there," learns that it is for a trifling misdemeanor, and that punishments are not generally severe; though the guide tells of one soldier who, he says, "threw his cap at the Colonel, and got five years for it; and we thought he 'd get ten."

From the ramparts the picture extending before us southeastwardly is very fine indeed, as, over the rusty houses shouldering each other up the hill so that we can almost look down the chimneys, we look out to the fortified islands and points, with the ocean beyond.

Point Pleasant, thickly wooded to the water's edge, hides the strangely beautiful inlet from the harbor known as the North West Arm, which cuts into the land for a distance of four miles (half a mile in width), suggesting a Norwegian fiord; but that, and the country all about the city, we enjoy in a long drive later.

On the return, regardless of the gaze of passengers astonished at our unconventional actions, we sit on the platform of the rear car, while

"Pleasantly gleams in the soft, sweet air the Basin of Minas,"

and the model conductor plies us with bits of information, which we devour with the avidity of cormorants.

GRAND PRÉ.

GRAND PRÉ.

FINALLY the brakeman shouts "Grand *Pree;*" and Octavia remarks, "Yes, indeed, this is the *grand prix* of our tour," as the party step off the train at this region of romance. The gallant conductor, with an air of mystery, leads the way to a storage-room in the little box of a station, and there chops pieces from a clay-covered plank and presents us as souvenirs. "Pieces of a coffin of one of the Acadians, exhumed at Grand Pré fourteen months ago, near the site of the old church," we are told; and when he continues: "A woman's bone was found in it," one unromantic and matter-of-fact member of the Octave asserts, "Evangeline's grandmother, of course;" while another sceptically remarks, "That's more than *I* can swallow; it would give me such a spell o' coughin' as I couldn't get over;" but the conductor and others staunchly avouch the genuineness of the article, affirming that they were present " when it was dug up."

The " forest primeval," if it ever stood in this region, must have clothed the distant hills which bound the vast meadow, and now are covered with a dense growth of small trees which are *not* " murmuring pines."

A superannuated tree in the distance it is said once shaded the smithy of " Basil Lajeunesse," that " mighty man of the village ; " and only stony hollows in the ground mark the site of the house of " Father Felician " and the village church.

It was to this spot, then, that the wondering peasants were lured by stratagem, when, —

> " with a summons sonorous
> Sounded the bell from its tower, and over the meadows a
>   drum beat.
> Thronged ere long was the church with men. Without in
>   the churchyard,
> Waited the women. They stood by the graves, and hung on
>   the head-stones
> Garlands of autumn-leaves and evergreens fresh from the
>   forest.
> Then came the guard from the ships, and marching proudly
>   among them

> Entered the sacred portal. With loud and dissonant clangor
> Echoed the sound of their brazen drums from ceiling to casement, —
> Echoed a moment only, and slowly the ponderous portal
> Closed, and in silence the crowd awaited the will of the soldiers."

After refreshing ourselves with pure, clear, and cold water from the old well, — made by the French, and re-walled a few years ago, — we turn away, with "a longing, lingering look behind," and continue our drive through the great prairie, which resembles the fertile meadow-land along the Connecticut River. We stop a few moments near a picturesque little church of gray unpainted wood, and look off over the verdant fields to the point where a distant shimmer of water catches the eye, and the hills bound the picture. Near at hand, on the right, the trunk of an aged apple-tree, "planted by the French," shows one green shoot; and about the church are Lombardy poplars, which, though good-sized trees, are perhaps only shoots from those planted by the Acadians, in remembrance of such arboreal grenadiers of their native land.

The old French dike is surmounted by a rough rail fence, and is now far inland, as hundreds of acres have been reclaimed beyond, —

"Dikes that the hands of the farmers had raised with labor
    incessant
Shut out the turbulent tides."

Our lamented American poet never visited this region which he describes so delightfully; his reason being that, cherishing an ideal picture, he feared reality might dissipate it. Yet an easy journey of twenty-eight hours would have brought him hither; and we, feeling confident that he could not have been disappointed, shall always regret that he did not come.

As an appropriate close to this sentimental journey, we drive through the secluded Gaspereau valley, along the winding river, which is hardly more than a creek, toward its wider part where it flows into the Basin, which stretches out broad and shining. With such a view before us, we cannot fail to picture mentally the tragic scenes of that October day in

1755, when the fleet of great ships lay in the Basin, and

"When on the falling tide the freighted vessels departed,
Bearing a nation, with all its household gods, into exile,
Exile without an end, and without an example in story;"

those whom Burke describes as "the poor, innocent, deserving people, whom our utter inability to govern or reconcile, gave us no sort of right to extirpate," were torn from their happy homes, and

"Scattered like dust and leaves, when the mighty blasts of October
Seize them, and whirl them aloft, and sprinkle them far o'er the ocean."

In the midst of these peaceful scenes was perpetrated a cruel wrong, and an inoffensive people banished by the mandate of a tyrant!

In that beautiful poem, parts of which one unconsciously "gets by heart," or falls into the habit of quoting when sojourning in this lovely region, Basil the blacksmith says: —

"Louisburg is not forgotten, nor Beau-Séjour nor Port Royal;"

and having held an impromptu history class on the subject of the last mentioned, we turn our attention to the other fortified points of which "the hasty and somewhat irascible" sledge-wielder spoke.

By the treaty of Utrecht in 1713 Acadia was ceded to the English; but the French colonists, in taking the oath of allegiance to their new rulers (1727-28), were promised that they should not be required at any time to take up arms against France. They were now in the position of Neutrals, and by that name were known; but this placed them in an awkward predicament, as they were suspected by both contending powers. The English hated them, believing their sympathies to be with the French; while even their countrymen in Canada were distrustful of them, urging them to withdraw.

The English colonists, fearing the extension of the French possessions, and having Puritanical aversion of Roman Catholicism, — of which the Neutrals were devout adherents, — entered upon the expedition against the French forts with the zeal of fanatics, seeming in some instances to consider their incursions in the light of religious crusades.

These "men whose lives glided on like rivers that water the woodlands," whose descendants are to this day childlike and simple-hearted, could not understand these political distinctions, and naturally clung to the pleasant farms which they had reclaimed from the sea and cultivated so diligently, being most reluctant, of course, to leave those

"Strongly built houses, with frames of oak and of chestnut,
Such as the peasants of Normandy built in the reign of the Henries.
Thatched were the roofs, with dormer-windows ; and gables projecting
Over the basement below protected and shaded the doorway."

The French dominions were guarded by a chain of forts extending all along the Atlantic coast, from the St. Lawrence to the Gulf of Mexico. That on Cape Breton Island, which protected the approach to the St. Lawrence, was considered invincible, its walls being thirty feet high, forty feet thick, and surrounded by a moat eighty feet in width.

Boston sent out a fleet of forty-one vessels and three thousand men to Cape Breton, to assail the "Gibraltar of America," as the fort of Louisburg was called. Forces from New Hampshire and Connecticut joined the expedition at Canso; and this remarkable fortress, whose fortifications alone cost five million dollars, was besieged, and capitulated after forty-nine days, yielding to untrained soldiers; the victory owing to "mere audacity and hardihood, backed by the rarest good luck," as one English writer says. The conquerors themselves were amazed at their success when they discovered the great strength of the fort. Their victory was, in fact, due largely to manœuvres which deceived the French regarding the strength of their forces.

This was ten years before the dispersion of the French Neutrals was effected; and during those years the Acadians, being zealous Catholics and devoted to the mother country, naturally but almost unconsciously were drawn into the disputes between France and England; and it is not to be wondered at, if, as some authorities state, there were three hundred of their young men found in arms when the English attacked Fort Beau-Séjour. The French had built Forts Beau-Séjour and Gaspereau on the neck connecting the peninsula of Nova Scotia with the mainland, to guard the entrance to their territory. A few hot-headed youths, who thought they were honestly serving their country and people by taking up arms in defence, might have been forgiven, particularly as it is known that some were pressed into the service, and that the oath which they had taken years before absolved them from taking arms against France, but did not pledge them against serving in her defence.

These forts were taken by Lieutenant-Colonel Moncton in June, 1755, the garrison of Beau-Séjour being sent to Louisburg on condition that they should not take up arms in America for six months. Prince Edward's Island — then called St. John's Island — fell into the hands of the English when Cape Breton was taken, and the inhabitants were sent to France. In the summer of 1755 matters seemed to be culminating, and the bitter dissensions were brought to a crisis. The Neutrals were again called upon to take the oath, the following being the form in which it was presented to them: "Je promets et jure sincerement, en foi de Chrétien, que je serai entierement fidele et obeirai vraiment sa Majesté Le Roi George, que je reconnais pour le Souverain seigneur de l'Acadie, ou nouvelle Ecosse — ainsi Dieu me soit en aide."

But this was not the "reserved oath," as the former one was called; and the Acadians, feeling themselves bound by the old pledge, asked exemption from this, and requested the restoration of arms which had been taken from them, agreeing also to keep faithfully the old form of oath.

Deputies from the settlements near Port Royal (which were above, below, and almost on the site of the present town of Annapolis), at Pisiquid (now Windsor), Minas, etc., were sent to Halifax, where a long conference was held; but the deputies still declining to accept the new oath, they were imprisoned, and the deportation of the Acadians decided upon. In order to do this artifice was resorted to, to prevent the people from suspecting what was in store for them, and that the poor peasants might have no chance to leave themselves or carry away their possessions. "Both old men and young men, as well as the lads of ten years of age," were called, by a proclamation, "to attend at the church at Grand Pré" at a certain time; and it was declared that "no excuse" would "be admitted, on any pretence whatever, on pain of forfeiting goods and chattels, in default of real estate."

The settlers on the Basin of Minas were immigrants from Saintonge, Poitou, and La Rochelle, who came to this country in the early part of the seventeenth century. The land which they had reclaimed from the Basin was rich and fertile; they exported grain to Boston, and became prosperous. The object of the call to the church does not seem to have been suspected. When Basil says, —

"Four days now are passed since the English ships at their anchors
Ride in the Gaspereau's mouth, with their cannon pointed against us.

What their designs may be is unknown; but all are com-
manded
On the morrow to meet in the church, where his Majesty's
mandate
Will be proclaimed as law in the land;"

Benedict responds, —

"Perhaps the harvests in England
By the untimely rains or untimelier heat have been blighted,
And from our bursting barns they would feed their cattle and
children."

But in the church the mystery was solved soon enough, and naturally a terrible scene ensued. They were informed that their "lands, tenements, cattle, and live-stock of all kinds were to be forfeited to the crown, with all their effects, saving their money and household goods," and they themselves banished; though, "so far as the capacity of the transports permitted," they were "to be allowed to carry their household goods with them." They were also promised that families should not be separated, and that the transportation should be made as easy as possible.

Then they were declared prisoners, and the

church became the guard-house. Ten men at a time were allowed to leave the building, to pack their goods and assist in the preparations for departure; and when they returned ten others were also permitted to leave for a time. While Moncton was destroying Remsheg, Shediac, and other towns on the Gulf coast, Handfield gathered up the French Annapolitans, and Murray those about Windsor, putting them on shipboard; and on the 21st of October the ships, with their wretched passengers, set sail. In the confusion and hurry of embarkation some families were separated; and it is on this fact that the story of Evangeline is founded.

Most of the exiles were scattered among the towns of Massachusetts; and in the State House in Boston some curious old records relate to them, one town desiring compensation "for keeping three French pagans," from which it seems that there was still prejudice against them because of their religion.

"From the cold lakes of the north to sultry southern
    Savannahs,"
to the region where

"On the banks of the Têche are the towns of St. Maur and
St. Martin,"

to the parish of Attakapas

"and the prairies of fair Opelousas"

in Louisiana, some of the exiles wandered. Their descendants live there at the present time, and are known as Cajeans. Though sometimes harshly treated in the towns where they were quartered, though shouldered off from one village to another when one grew weary of or made excuses for not maintaining them, the poor wanderers were mild, gentle, and uncomplaining.

A writer in "Canadian Antiquities" says: "None speaks the tongue of Evangeline; and her story, though true as it is sweet and sorrowful, is heard no more in the scenes of her early days."

The way in which it came about that Longfellow wrote his poem was in this wise: one day, when Hawthorne and a friend from Salem were dining with the poet, the Salem gentleman remarked to the host, "I have been trying to persuade Hawthorne to write a story based on a legend of Acadie and still current there, — the legend of a girl who, in the dispersion of the Acadians, was separated from her lover, and passed her life in waiting and seeking for him, and only found him dying in a hospital when both were old." The host, surprised that this romance did not strike the fancy of the novelist, asked if he himself might use it for a poem; and Hawthorne, readily assenting, promised not to attempt the subject in prose until the poet had tried what he could do with it in metrical form. No one rejoiced more heartily in the success of the world-renowned poem than the writer who generously gave up an opportunity to win fame from his working up of the sad theme.

Authorities differ widely regarding the number of persons expelled from Acadia, many historians giving the estimate at seven thousand. In a letter from Governor Lawrence to the governors of the different colonies to which the exiles were sent, he says: "As their numbers amount to near seven thousand persons, the driving them off with leave to go whither they pleased would have doubtless strengthened Canada with so considerable a number of inhabitants." Bryant says: "Seven thousand probably represented with sufficient accuracy the total French population of Acadia in 1755; but the entire number of the exiled did not exceed, if Minot be correct, two thousand, of whom many subsequently returned to Acadia."

Five years after the departure of the exiles a fleet of twenty-two vessels sailed from Connecticut for Grand Pré with a large number of colonists, who took possession of the deserted farms. They found sixty ox carts and yokes, while on the edge of woods of the inland country and in sheltered places heaps of bones told of cattle which had perished of starvation and cold after their owners were forced to leave them to such a fate. A few straggling families of the Acadians were also found, who had escaped from the search of the soldiers, and had lived in hiding in the wilds of the back country for five years, and during that time had not tasted bread.

CLARE.

CLARE.

"Only along the shore of the mournful and misty Atlantic
Linger a few Acadian peasants, whose fathers from exile
Wandered back to their native land to die in its bosom.
In the fisherman's cot the wheel and the loom are still
    busy,
Maidens still wear their Norman caps and their kirtles of
    homespun,
And by the evening fire repeat Evangeline's story."

Resolved to see these curious "Clare settlements," extending for fifty miles on the coast, where descendants of the French Acadians live in peace and unity, we reluctantly take our departure at last from dear old Annapolis, which has been our restful haven so long, and where we have been reviving school-days in studying history and geography seasoned with poetry and romance. Although it was expected that the W. C. R. R. would be completed from Yarmouth to Annapolis by the latter part of 1876, we are pleased to find that this is not the case, and that we shall have to take steamer, train, and carriage to our destination; anticipating that any place so out of the beaten track must be interesting.

The French settlements, a succession of straggling hamlets, were founded by descendants of the exiles, who, —

> "a raft as it were from the shipwrecked nation, . . .
> Bound by the bonds of a common belief and a common misfortune,"

drifted back to "L'Acadie" in 1763, the year of the treaty between France and England.

The lands of their fathers in their old haunts on the Basin of Minas were in possession of people from New England; and, having a natural and inherited affection for localities by the sea, they wandered down the coast and scattered along shore as we find them now.

A pleasant excursion by steamer to Digby, thence proceeding some miles by rail, finally a long but charming drive by the shore of St. Mary's Bay, and we are set down at the house of a family of the better class, among these kindly and old-fashioned farming and fisher folk.

This beautiful bay is thirty-five miles long, was christened Baie St. Marie by Champlain, and here the four ships of De Monts lay in calm and secure harbor for two weeks in 1604, while the adventurers were examining the shores of Nova Scotia, — explorations in which the discovery of iron pyrites deluded them with the belief that this would prove an El Dorado.

Madame M. at first looks dismayed at the appearance of such a group of strangers at her door, and is sure she cannot accommodate us; but her daughters slyly jog her elbow, saying something in an undertone, as if urging her to consent, and we are made most comfortable.

At first the family are a little shy, but in a couple of days we become quite well acquainted; and, when the time comes for our departure they "wish we could stay longer,"— a wish which we heartily re-echo.

Madame proudly displays her treasures in hand-spun and home-woven linen and blankets; also a carpet, the material for which she first spun, then dyed, and finally wove; and, though it has been in use for ten years, it is still fresh and shows no apparent wear. In response to our entreaties, she shows us the loom, and brings out her spinning-wheel to instruct us in that housewifely accomplishment. How easy it looks, as the fleecy web moves through her fingers, and winds in smooth, even yarn on the swiftly-turning reel; and, oh, what bungling and botching when we essay that same! The two pretty, modest, and diffident daughters are quite overcome at last, and join in our peals of merriment.

One — oh bliss! — is named *Evangeline*, and, if we understand correctly, there is an old name similar* to this among these people. Though they sing some charming old French chansons for us, the two sweet girls cannot be induced to converse in that language. Madame laughs, saying, "Dey know dey doant speak de *goot* French, de fine French, so dey will only talk Angleesh wid you." But in the evening, when Octavia sings an absurd college song, with a mixture of French and English words, they enjoy the fun; and immediately set to work to learn: —

"Oh, Jean Baptiste, pourquoi vous grease
  My little dog's nose with tar?
  Madame, je grease his nose with tar
  Because he have von grand catarrh;
  Madame, je grease his nose
  Parcequ'il he vorries my leetle fite chat."

Then the pretty Evangeline in turn becomes instructor, the theme being an ancient peasant song of France which her grandmother used to sing. One plays the melody from memory, while the other hastily rules a bit of paper and writes off the notes, afterwards copying the words from a scrap of tattered manuscript; and thus the lady from "America" feels that she has secured a pretty souvenir of the visit:

LES PERLES ET LES ÉTOILES.

The word "*mensongès*" has not the meaning in French which our literal translation would give it. It probably signifies the pretty falsehoods or white lies to which lovers are somewhat addicted. The next day is Sunday, and troops of people, in their peculiar costume, appear on the road from all directions, wending their way to the great white wooden church.

Despite the innate grace of the French, of which we hear so much, we see that the young men among these peasants are not unlike the shy and awkward country lads of Yankeeland. Before and between the services they roost on the fence opposite the church, while the young girls — totally oblivious of their proximity, of course — gather in groups on the other side of the road, gossiping. We infer that many have come a long distance to attend service, as we see several families eating their lunch, picnic fashion, in the fields near the church. In the church, what a sensation the strangers make, and how interesting is the service! To one of us, at least, the grand service of Notre Dame of Paris was not so impressive as this. In the one case, a famous Bishop, robed in priceless lace and cloth of gold, with a troop of acolytes at the altar, while the most famous singers of the Opera filled the vast structure with rapturous melody; in the other, a large plain wooden building with glaring windows of untinted glass; the priest in vestments of coarse Nottingham lace and yellow damask, — but with spiritual, benignant countenance, — and a choir of untrained voices. A company of men droned out Gregorian chants in painfully nasal tones, using antique books with square-headed notes; then the sweet voice of our host's daughter, Evangeline, sounded solo, and her youthful companions in the choir took up the chorus of the Kyrie Eleison: —

"Then came the evening service. The tapers gleamed from the altar,
Fervent and deep was the voice of the priest, and the people responded,
Not with their lips alone, but with their hearts; and the Ave Maria
Sang they, and fell on their knees, and their souls with devotion translated,
Rose on the ardor of prayer, like Elijah ascending to heaven."

The young girls array themselves in hats and costumes which are only two or three years behind the prevailing mode; but the attire of the middle-aged and elderly women is striking and peculiar. For Sundays, this is invariably black throughout, and yet does not look funereal. The dress is of plain bombazine or alpaca, a shawl folded square, and over the head a large silk handkerchief, which must be put on with greatest exactness and care to make just so many folds at the sides with a huge knot under the chin; while the point at the back hangs below the neck, and generally has one or more initials neatly worked in colors ("cross-stitch") in the corner. As most have clear olive complexion, with rich color in the cheeks, and lustrous black eyes, this head-dress is surprisingly becoming, giving quite a gypsyish effect.

During the week, a calico dress with long white apron is worn by women and children, and over the head a light chintz handkerchief, or a gay "bandanna;" — quite suggestive of the every-day wear of foreign peasantry. We are told that a girl's wealth is sometimes estimated by the number of handkerchiefs she owns. Mrs. R. says she has, in winter, seen a girl divest herself of no less than ten head-kerchiefs; taking them off, one by one, and carefully folding them in the most natural manner, as if there could be nothing uncommon or amusing in the proceeding.

The old women, in winter, wear enormous cloaks, made with a large square yoke, into which eight or ten breadths of material are closely plaited, — this unwieldy garment completely enveloping them from head to foot.

These distinctive features in costume are disappearing, and ere long our American peasantry may become commonplace and uninteresting. Let us hope that they may never lose the sweet simplicity, frankness, honesty, thrift, and other pleasing characteristics which they now possess.

In the houses is seen a peculiar rocking-settle, similar to those in use among the Pennsylvania Dutch. This odd piece of furniture has one end railed in front to serve for cradle;

so papa, mamma, and baby can rock and "take comfort" together.

Towards evening we visit the convent, where the sisters — who probably do not receive frequent calls from visitors — seem glad of the opportunity for a pleasant chat and a bit of news from the outside world. They show us through their exquisitely neat establishment, where, in the culinary department, a crone who is deaf and rather childish approaches us with such strong evidence of delight, that we expect at least to be embraced; but a sign from the Superior relieves us from the impending demonstration.

At sunset, as we stroll along the road, three pretty little girls who are driving home a flock of geese tempt us to air our French a little, and a lively conversation ensues, causing their black eyes to sparkle and their white teeth to flash bewitchingly. One of the children explains why one of the awkward birds wears a clumsy triangular collar of wood, with a stake apparently driven through its throat, "to prevent it from going through the fences;" and when one of the strangers, imitating the waddling gait of the creatures, improvises, —

> Bon soir,
> Madame Oie,
> Veux tu le blé ?
> Il est à toi !

such a shout of merry laughter is heard as one might willingly go a long way to listen to. When one gives her name, "Thérese *le Blanc*," our query, "Votre père, est il *la Notaire ?*" strange to say, puzzles her; but she probably is not familiar with a certain famous poem, although our hostess and her daughters have perused it.

As time passes, and she feels better acquainted and at ease with us, Madame M.'s younger daughter amuses us by showing some mischievous tendency; and we conclude she is something of "a tease." In the most artless manner, and without intentional familiarity, she slides her arm through Octavia's in a confidential manner and imparts some important information "dans l'oreille." What is it? Well, remember it is *whispered ;* and now *don't* go and tell! It is that there *is* a swain who is Evangeline's special devoted; and the quick blush which rises most becomingly on that damsel's cheek speaks for itself. We have seen for ourselves how

"Many a youth, as he knelt in the church and opened his missal
 Fixed his eyes upon her;"

and as our eyes turn to the lovely view of the Bay with its sheltering highlands we can readily imagine how, on just such evenings as this, —

"apart, in the twilight gloom of a window's embrasure,
Sat the lovers, and whispered together, beholding the moon rise
Over the pallid sea,"

while

"Silently one by one, in the infinite meadows of heaven,
 Blossom the lovely stars, the forget-me-nots of the angels."

We do not ask if the lover's name is "Gabriel," but earnestly wish her a happier lot than that of the sad heroine of Grand Pré's story.

The sun sinks behind the hills which bound lovely St. Mary's Bay, and we plainly see the two curious openings known as the Grand Passage and Petit Passage, through which the fishermen sail when conveying their cargoes to St. John. The Petit Passage is one mile wide; and passing through this deep strait the hardy fishermen can, in favorable weather, cross to St. John in eight to ten hours. These highlands across the Bay, known as Digby Neck and Long Island, are a continuation of the range of mountains terminating in Blomidon on the Minas Basin, and so singularly cut away to make entrance to Annapolis Basin, at St. George's Channel, vulgarly known as Digby Gut.

When De Monts and his party were ready to continue their cruise from this sheltered haven, behold! one of their company — a priest — was missing; and though they waited several days, making signals and firing guns, such sounds were drowned by the roar of the surf, and never reached the ears of the poor man lost in the woods. At last, supposing that the wanderer had fallen a prey to wild animals, the explorers sailed away, and, finding the entrance to Annapolis Basin, began to make preparation for colonizing at Port Royal.

Sixteen days after the disappearance of the priest, some of De Monts's men returning to this Bay to examine the minerals more thoroughly, were attracted by a signal fluttering on the shore, and, hurrying to land, there found the poor priest, emaciated and exhausted. What strange sensations the distracted wanderer must have experienced in these forest wilds, with starvation staring him in the face! No charms did *he* see in this scene which now delights us; and doubtless, with Selkirk, would have exclaimed, "Better dwell in the midst of alarms, than to live in this beautiful place."

This strange wild coast and the Cod Banks of Newfoundland were known to and visited by foreign fishermen at a very early date. "The Basques, that primeval people, older than history," frequented these shores; and it is supposed that such fisheries existed even before the voyage of Cabot (1497). There is strong evidence of it in 1504; while in 1527 fourteen fishing vessels — Norman, Portuguese, and Breton — were seen at one time in the Bay of Fundy, near the present site of St. John.

When we question our hostess as to the species of finny tribes found in these waters, she mentions menhaden, mackerel, alewives, herring, etc.; and, proud of her English, concludes her enumeration with, "Dat is de most only feesh dey kotch here."

Another drive of many miles along the shore brings us to the neighborhood of the very jumping-off place of the Scotian peninsula, with novel sights to attract the attention *en route*. Now and then a barn with thatched roof; here a battered boat overturned to make Piggy and family a habitation; there heavy and lumbering *three*-wheeled carts, with the third rotator placed between the shafts, so the poor ox who draws the queer vehicle has n't much room to spare.

Huge loads of hay pass us, and other large farm-wagons, drawn invariably by handsome oxen. The ox-yokes are a constant marvel to us; 'for, divested of the bows, they are fastened with leather straps to the bases of the poor creatures' horns. Evidently there is no "S. P. C. A." here; and we cannot convince those with whom we converse on the subject that the poor animals would pull better by their shoulders than by their heads. At several places we see the clumsiest windmills for sawing wood: not after the fashion of the picturesque buildings which Don Quixote so valiantly opposed, but a heavy frame-work or scaffolding about twelve feet in height. To this is attached a wheel of heaviest plank with five fans, each one shaped like the arm of a Greek cross, and the whole so ponderous we are confident that nothing less than a hurricane could make it revolve.

Here is a house entirely covered with diamond-shaped shingles, having also double and triple windows, which are long, narrow, and pointed at the top, yet not suggestive of the gothic.

Next we pass a point where an old post-inn once stood, and where the curiously curved, twisted, and strangely complicated iron frame which once held the swinging sign still remains.

Many a bleak ride did that mounted carrier have, no doubt, in days of yore; and we can imagine him saying:—

"The night is late, I dare not wait; the winds begin to blow,
And ere I gain the rocky plain there'll be a storm, I know!"

At our final halting-place all is bustle, in preparation for a two days' fête, which commences next day; nevertheless, had we been princes of the realm, we could not have been shown truer hospitality. Père Basil Armand himself waits upon us, while his wife is cooking dainties for the coming festival; and the pretty Monica, giving up her neat apartment to one of our party, lodges at a neighbor's.

Monsieur R., though seventy-eight years of age, retains all his faculties perfectly, is straight as an Indian, his luxuriant hair unstreaked with gray, and he is over six feet in height. He reminds us of the description of Benedict Bellefontaine:—

"Stalwart and stately in form was the man of seventy winters;
Hearty and hale was he, an oak that is covered with snow-flakes;"

but our host is even a finer specimen of vigorous age. Then his books — for he is collector of customs, a post which he has held for twenty-five years — would amaze many a younger clerk or scribe; and he is amused, but apparently gratified, when we ask for his autograph, which he obligingly writes for each in a firm, clear, and fine hand. He says of the people of this settlement, that they generally speak patois, though many, like himself, can speak pure French; that they are faithful and true-hearted, industrious and thrifty. He adds: "We are not rich, we are not poor, but we are happy and contented."

During the fearful scenes of 1793 an amiable priest of great culture, a man noble in character, as by birth, fled from the horrors of the French Revolution, and found among this simple, child-like people a peaceful haven and happy home. This earnest man, Abbé Ségoigne, devoted himself in every way to their good, governing them wisely and well, and might truly have said, in the words of Father Felician, —

"I labored among you and taught you, not in word alone but in deed."

Many years he resided here. His memory is now venerated almost as that of a saint, and we are of course greatly interested when Monsieur R. brings out, with just pride, his greatest treasure, — a cumbersome and quaint old volume which was once the property of the good priest.

There is a strong feeling of brotherhood, like the Scottish clanship, among the people; and the lands of parents are divided and subdivided, so the children at marriage may each receive a portion as dower, and "settle down" near their childhood's home; consequently the farms are "long drawn out," extending sometimes in very narrow strips for a mile or more inland.

Abbé Raynal writes most poetically, although not absolutely in rhyme, of this gentle brotherhood, "where every misfortune was relieved before it could be felt, without ostentation on the one hand and without meanness on the other. Whatever slight differences arose from time to time among them were amicably adjusted by their elders."

Our driver says "étwelles" for *étoiles*, "fret" for *froid*, "si" for *oui*, etc.; the dancing crests of the waves he calls "chapeaux blancs," which is similar to our appellation, and also speaks of "un bon *coop* de thé," showing that an English word is occasionally adopted, though hardly recognizable in their peculiar phraseology.

Our pleasant acquaintance, Dr. R., who lived here several years after he "came out" from England, tells us that the mackerouse, a wild duck, is found here; and, as it subsists upon fish, the people are allowed to eat that bird on Fridays. He also says that the pigs wade out into the mud at low tide to root for clams; while the crows, following in their tracks, steal the coveted shell-fish from under the very noses of the swine. Of the remarkably long nasal appendages of this peculiar porcine species he adds, "They do say that they'll root under a fence and steal potatoes from the third row!"

In this locality we hear Yarmouth spoken of as if it were a port equal to New York in importance, and so it doubtless seems to these simple untravelled people. In reality it is a prosperous maritime town owning one hundred and thirty thousand tons of shipping, and is a mildly picturesque place when the tide is high.

The Indian name appropriately signifies " end of the land," and one might naturally suppose, when arriving there, that he had reached "that famous fabled country, 'away down east;'" though, should he continue his travels to Labrador, that mythical region would still lure him on. The inhabitants are mainly seafaring men, — many of the captains of Cape Ann fishing fleets came from here originally, — and they call the Atlantic from Cape Ann to Yarmouth all Bay of Fundy, though that is "rather stretching it."

It was near here that De Monts made his first landing and caught a nightingale (May 16, 1604). Not far beyond, about the shores of Argyle Bay, a great many "French Neutrals" found refuge in 1755 (though an English ship tried to rout them); and they were hunted like wild animals about here for two or three years after.

We conclude that the hamlets on the upper part of St. Mary's Bay are most interesting, and that it is hardly worth while to continue down the coast unless one desires to take steamer from this port to Boston.

In our strolls about the village, we come to a point on the shore where a boy has a quantity of fine large lobsters which he has just taken from the trap; and when one of our party asks for what price he will sell some, the answer — "One cent each" — is so astounding that the query is repeated, so we may be convinced that we have heard aright. Père Basil is evidently surprised at our taste when he sees us returning with our purchases, as he remarks, "We don't think much of those at this time of year;" from which we infer that at some seasons they have to depend so much upon fish, lobsters, etc., that they become weary of them.

There is such Gallic atmosphere about this place (and trip) that Octavia is infected, and perpetrates doggerel on a postal, which is to be mailed from the "land's end" to acquaint foreign relatives with our advent in a foreign country also! —

        Tout est "O. K."
        Je suis arrivée
        Dans ce joli pays,
        Avec bonne santé,
        Mais bien fatiguée.

Adieu.   E. B. C.
(O quelle atrocité!
Mais je n'ai ni grammaire
Ni dictionnaire français.)

"Pleasantly rose next morn the sun,"

and though we are up and out betimes, —

"Life had long been astir in the village, and clamorous labor
 Knocked with its hundred hands at the golden gate of the
   morning.
 Now from the country around, from the farms and the
   neighboring hamlets,
 Came in their holiday dresses the blithe Acadian peasants.
 Many a glad good morrow and jocund laugh from the young
   folk
 Made the bright air brighter, as up from the numerous
   meadows,
 Group after group appeared, and joined or passed on the
   highway.
 Long ere noon, in the village all sounds of labor were
   silenced.
 Thronged were the streets with people; and noisy groups
   at the house-doors
 Sat in the cheerful sun, and rejoiced and gossiped together.
 Every house was an inn, where all were welcomed and
   feasted;
 For with this simple people, who lived like brothers together,
 All things were held in common, and what one had was
   another's."

Père Basil is surprised to find that we have not come especially to attend the festival, of which we had not heard until our arrival, though he evidently thinks the fame of their elaborate preparations has travelled far and wide. While we are waiting for the vehicles which are to convey us to the railroad station (a long drive inland) many most picturesque groups pass the door; some walking, some riding on ox-carts, and all carrying flowers, pyramidal and gorgeously ornamented cakes, or curious implements for games, totally unknown to us moderns! Our host has a pleasant greeting for all, and receives cordial reply, and sometimes merry jest and repartee from the happy revellers.

Much to our delight, our route to the station passes the grounds where the fête is held; and here we see booths of boughs, a revolving swing (which they call a "galance"), fluttering flags, and gay banners.

Merry groups of young people are engaged in games or dances, while the elders are gossiping, or look on approvingly, and the air is filled with lively music. Can it be that the melodies which we hear are the famous old ones, "Tous les Bourgeois de Chartres" and "Le Carillon de Dunkerque"? It would hardly surprise us, as this quaint place seems a century or so behind the times.

We wish we could stop for an hour or two to watch them; but trains wait for no man, and we must return to Digby and there take steamer for St. John.

That short passage of twelve leagues has been our bugbear for some days, as travellers whom we met at Annapolis pictured its horrors so vividly, representing its atrocities as exceeding those of the notorious English Channel. Yet we glide as smoothly through the eddies and whirlpools of the beautiful Gap as a Sound steamer passes through Hell Gate. This remarkable passage-way is two miles in length; the mountains rise on either hand to the height of five hundred and sixty and six hundred and ten feet, the tide between rushing at the rate of five knots an hour. We note gray, water-worn rocks at the sides, resembling pumice in appearance, though of course very much harder stone, and evidently of similar formation to that of the ovens at Mt. Desert. And now we sweep quietly out into the dreaded Bay of Fundy, the water of which rests in such oily quietude as even Long Island Sound rarely shows. On this hazy, lazy, sunny afternoon not a swell is perceptible (unless some among the passengers might be designated by that title); and after four and a half hours of most dreamy navigation, we enter the harbor of St. John, where the many-tinted signal lights are reflected in the black water, and a forest fire on a distant hill throws a lurid light over the scene.

When the tide turns, there can be seen frequently far out in the Bay a distinct line in the water, — a line as sharply defined as that between the Arve and Rhone at their junction near Geneva. It is when wind and tide are at variance that the roughest water is encountered; and they say that if one would avoid an unpleasant game of pitch and toss, the passage across should not be attempted during or immediately after a blow from the northwest or southeast. So make a note of that! Old salts at Annapolis told us that the water of the Bay " gets up" suddenly, but also quiets down soon, and that after a windless night one might be reasonably certain of a comfortable trip across.

Having supposed that St. John had lost half its charm and quaintness since the fire, we are surprised to find so much of interest when we are out at the "top of the morning" next day, and are reluctant to leave; but here the Octave disintegrates, scatters to finish the season elsewhere; and each member, on arrival at home, probably invests in reams of paper and quarts of ink, setting to work to tell his friends all about it, and where "they must surely go next summer!"

"L'ISLE DES MONTS DESERTS."

"L'ISLE DES MONTS DESERTS."

(A LETTER BY THE WAY.)

"Beautiful Isle of the Sea!"

WHEN we said, "Let us go to Mt. Desert," Joe gave us Punch's advice on marriage: "Don't!" Sue said, "It has lost half its charms by becoming so fashionable;" and Hal added, as an unanswerable argument, "You'll not be able to get enough to eat." As to his veracity on this subject we cannot vouch, though we can testify to his voracity, and mischievously throw a quotation at him: —

"The turnpike to men's hearts, I find,
Lies through their mouths, or I mistake mankind."

Despite such discouragements, being naturally obstinate, go we do; and here we are in the most refreshingly primitive and unfashionable abiding place, the domicile commanding a view which cannot be equalled by any public house on the island. From the piazzas and our windows the eye never tires of gazing on the beautiful bay with its numerous islands, — a charming picture, with the blue and symmetrical range of Gouldsboro' hills for background. From a point not far back of the house, the eye ranges from the head of Frenchman's Bay out to the broad ocean; while a retrospective view takes in the wild mountainous region of the interior of this lovely isle.

We arrive at a fortunate time. For a long while previous Nature had persistently enveloped her face in a veil, giving an air of mystery which the summer guests did not appreciate. The skipper of the yacht which conveys us when we circumnavigate the island tells us "there is a fog factory near by," a statement which, for a few days, we are inclined to credit. The nabobs of Newport, the Sybarites of Nahant, and even the commonplace rusticators at other shore resorts have been served in the same manner, however; so we sympathize with them fully, and with them exult at the final dissolution of the vapors, as the gray curtain gradually lifts and rolls away, its edge all jagged as if torn by the lance-like tips of fir and spruce trees as it swept over them. These noble hills are densely wooded, but not with the forest giants one sees among the White Mountains; and when I express my surprise thereat, I am told that fifty or sixty years ago the greater part of the island was denuded by fire, so that remains of the primeval forest can only be found in distant spots not easily accessible. Notices are now posted in the woods at various points, by which " visitors are earnestly requested to extinguish all fires which they may light, and not to strip the bark from the birches."

In our inland excursions the rugged mountains, with their storm-scarred, rocky summits, wild ravines, and forest-embedded bases, so constantly suggest the grand scenery of New Hampshire that we can hardly realize that we are anywhere near the sea. Then, on a sudden turn of the road, a broad stretch of ocean — blue, sparkling, and sail-dotted, framed in graceful birches, feathery larches, and dark pines — comes upon us as a surprise.

The peculiar vehicle which is here known as a " buckboard " we find a comfortable conveyance, with a motion which seems a combination of see-saw and baby-jumper. The " body " is composed of four long boards laid side by side, supported only at the extreme ends where they are hung over the axles. The seats are in the middle. They are neither elegant nor graceful, but easy, " springy " vehicles, which, having neither sides nor top covers, give unimpeded views, and are excellent for sight-seeing, though not precisely the thing for rainy weather.

Canoing is a favorite amusement; and in the management of these light and graceful boats many of the summer guests become quite expert. The motion suggests that of a gondola. A catamaran scoots about the harbor among the islands; tiny steamers, sailing craft of all kinds, are seen; and sometimes United States training ships sail majestically into the bay and drop anchor, giving a finishing touch to the picture.

Skippers are very cautious, and frequently will not allow their canoes or other boats to go out, although it may appear perfectly safe to the uninitiated. Visitors rarely have any idea what sudden "flaws" and gusts of air are caused by the position of and openings between the mountains; and when these, as well as the tidal swell and currents of the ocean about the shore, have to be studied, navigation becomes scientific.

The arrival of the steamer is the great event of the day; and on Sunday, after morning service, the butterflies of fashion flit to the pier to see the landing of passengers. It is rather embarrassing for weary travellers to be obliged to "run the gauntlet" as they pass through the gay throng, for every one stares with all his might. This does not seem to be considered rude here, and every one is met by a "battery of eyes;" I presume because each person expects, if he remain here through the season, to meet every one whom he ever knew.

The yachting and tennis costumes which are worn here would certainly cause many of the sober residents of the Quaker City to open their eyes wide with horror, — if they were able to open them, and were not blinded by the first glance. One divinity, in scarlet and white striped awning-cloth, we christen the "mint stick." And *such* hats! — each so placed upon the head that, however huge, it is utterly useless as a shade; but as effect is what all are striving for, any other consideration is of no importance whatever. Such attire would be hooted at in some places; and we wonder that it does not strike old settlers breathless with amazement at the extravagances and follies of "these city folks." Jim quotes, "Any color so it's red," when surveying a brilliantly attired company at this place, as that aggressive hue prevails. These fantastic costumes are frequently seen in the mornings on the shore, where the wearers are engaged in an amusement here known as "rocking." This consists in lounging on the rocks with interesting youths, who, arrayed in picturesque yachting or tennis suits, pose artistically, and, beneath the shade of scarlet or Japanese umbrellas, talk of — the weather, of course. Elsewhere this would be known as flirting.

We do not approve of the names of some of

the public houses, and wonder that they could not have chosen more suggestive titles. The "Hotel des Isles" has a more suitable and appropriate cognomen, — if they would spell it correctly, which they invariably do not. This name is borne by descendants of the old French settlers, but is now, sad to tell, pronounced by their contemporaries " De Sizzle." We call our house Pleasant Haven, or Restful Retreat, though it appears under a different title in the guide-book. It would never do to tell what its name " really and truly " is, lest you should think I have been engaged to " puff " it. We have delicious bread and excellent fare ; and, though this is plain, of course, all is temptingly served, and everything neat and nice enough for any one.

Our rooms are extremely plain, but neat. Closets are unknown ; but on hooks along the wall on one side of the apartment we hang our garments, protecting them with chintz curtains which we brought for the purpose. A resident of Fifth Avenue occupies the garret-rooms above, having selected them from choice ;

and, expatiating on their advantages in quiet, air, and views, becomes an Attic Philosopher.

Occasionally we get out our fineries, and go to some " hop" or entertainment in the village, but return better satisfied with our present home; and, snapping our fingers at Mrs. Grundy, do not envy any of her votaries. If our advice were asked, we should say: "Come to one of the smaller hostelries, like this, where you can be independent and comfortable; and bring half-worn winter garments, with boots ditto, to be prepared for tramping and excursions."

The excursions which can be taken I will not enumerate; will merely state that the ascent of Green Mountain, in clear weather, and the drive to Great Head are most satisfactory. On our way to the latter point we stop at Anemone Cave, where we enjoy an impromptu concert by members of Philadelphia glee clubs, the fine voices and beautiful harmonies being enhanced by the dark arch of rock and the ceaseless music of the surf, which forms a grand accompaniment.

The view from Green Mountain is quite unique, the eye traversing ocean and land for forty miles in any direction; following the singularly serrated coast of Maine, the course of Somes Sound, — that remarkable inlet from the sea which almost divides the island, — and tracing the waving line of far distant mountain ranges. The mainland is curiously cut into long rocky points and ragged peninsulas, from which the islands seem to have broken off and drifted out to sea. From this height (fifteen hundred and thirty-five feet) the ocean seems placid and smooth, — much less awe-inspiring than from the shore, where the surges roll in with such tremendous power, as if endeavoring to crush the towering cliffs which oppose them. The clustering buildings of Bar Harbor appear like a child's playthings, or Nuremberg toys; the miniature vessels like sea-gulls just alighted; the white tents of the Indian encampment ludicrously suggest a laundry with big "wash" hung out to dry; and the whole scene looks as if viewed through the large end of an opera glass. It is a peaceful and beautiful picture for memory to treasure and look back upon with delight.

At Fernald's Point, at the base of Flying Mountain, two miles north of Southwest Harbor, is the supposed location of the French settlement, which was founded by a party of priests and colonists sent out from France to Port Royal (now Annapolis, Nova Scotia), who, losing their way in fog, landed here. The peaceful little community, after only a few weeks' occupancy, were routed by that grasping individual, Argall, the deputy-governor of Virginia, who was detested by his own colonists for his tyranny and rapacity. That person, not content with the domains which his position entitled him to govern, cruised along the Atlantic coast, making many such incursions among the colonists. In this case, after destroying the buildings, he cruelly set adrift in an open boat fifteen of the poor, harmless people, who, after suffering great hardships, were picked up by a trading vessel and conveyed to St. Malo. We wonder that investigations have not been made ere this at this spot, as it seems probable that old implements and

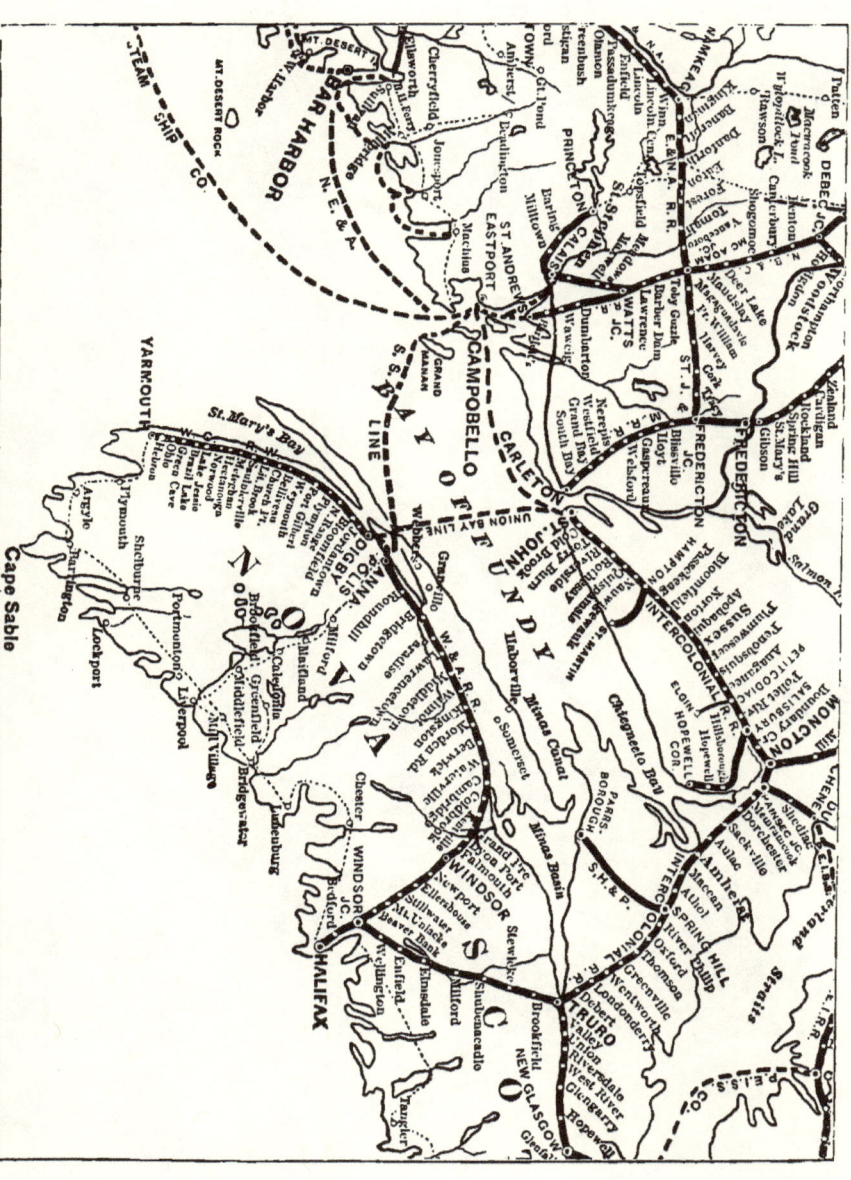

Map of the Acadian Region.

objects of interest might be brought to light. How we wish we were members of the Maine Historical Society, and by that body empowered to superintend excavations at the site of a colony which was in existence (1613) seven years before the landing of the Pilgrims!

Samuel de Champlain, friend, associate, and pilot of De Monts in the latter's investigations of his possessions in Acadia (in 1604), was sponsor of this island which has since become so famous, of which he speaks as " La grande Isle des Monts Deserts; " and by the early Lord of the Realm the whole of Frenchman's Bay was also called La Havre du Saint Sauveur. That wicked Jim says that the *Indian* name of the island must suggest itself to some travellers on their way here, unless they come by the land route.

There are thirty-five guests in our house, who form a pleasant company; and though of course there is great diversity of taste and character shown among them, they form a harmonious assembly. In the evenings we have "sings," readings, games, and charades, frequently growing hilarious. Sedate professors, dignified divines, and learned writers enter into these sports with the zest of schoolboys on a holiday. Some of these games may be new; and that others may derive amusement for similar occasions, I will describe two of them. In one, called Comparison, the company seat themselves in a circle. Each one whispers to his right-hand neighbor the name of a person (known to the company); to the one at his left, the name of an object. Then each in turn gives aloud the name which his neighbor whispered to him, and tells why he or she resembles the object, making the comparison complimentary or otherwise. The uncomplimentary comparisons are generally the most laughable, and of course all understand that 't is " all for fun," so no one takes any offence. For instance: " Mr. J. resembles the *harbor bar*, or did this morning, because there was a heavy swell rolling over him; " the company understanding this as an allusion to a frolicsome tussle which Mr. J. had with the beau of the house. A rhyming game also affords much amusement. One person gives his neighbor a list of words, — the words ending the lines of a sonnet or part of a poem, — and the person receiving the list must fill in the lines, bringing in the words given, in proper order, at the ends of the lines. In the following instance the words italicized are the ones which the player received from his neighbor; in this case the terminal words of Longfellow's beautiful description of a calm night by the sea will be recognized, although the word "ocean" was inadvertently substituted for "organ:" —

> "All the long white beach is *silent*
> As a beach should ever *be*,
> While the sea-gulls stand and *listen*
> To the moaning of the *sea*.
> All the solemn oysters *gather*,
> Gazing upward to the *sky*,
> While a lobster breaks the *silence*,
> Crooning low his *litany*.
> Little shrimps in their dark *caverns*,
> Eating supper all *alone*,
> Looking out upon the ocean,
> Whispering in an *undertone:*
> ''T is sad and lonely by these *beaches*,
> Shall we never go *beyond?*'
> All the barnacles, *uprising*,
> 'Never,' tearfully *respond*."

As we are by the sea, nautical rhymes seem to turn out naturally. The writer of this remarkable effusion is evidently not an evolutionist, though he may think there are some "queer fish" among the heterogeneous inhabitants of this island.

At last the day comes when we must turn away from these lovely scenes; and it is with regret, and many a backward look, that we are conveyed to the Rockland boat. That vessel pursues a circuitous route along the coast, among the picturesque islands; the trip suggesting quite forcibly the St. Lawrence with its Thousand Isles, as old Neptune is fortunately in amiable mood, and shows a smiling countenance. So we have no grudge to lay up against him, and only pictures tinged with *couleur-de-rose* to carry away with us.

SEA-SIDE AMUSEMENT IN THE "CITY OF SOLES."

As it is our custom to come to these New-England shores every summer, in order, as Jim says, to get salted so that we may keep well through the winter (by which you need not infer that we "get into a pickle"), we commence the process at this place, before proceeding to more Northerly points.

As the "dry spell" has made the roads so dusty that there is little pleasure in driving, and our horses are at present in the stables of our *Chateaux-en-Espagne*, and consequently not available this warm evening, we gather on the porch to be entertained by the learned converse of the professors, until an approaching storm drives us in-doors. Within the "shooting-box," as the young man who has travelled christens the house, — thinking that an appropriate title for a domicile where so many members of the Hunt family are collected, — there is a motley assembly, as they gather around the sitting-room table. There are Portuguese, Michiganders, Pennites, Illinoisyones, Bangorillas, and other specimens of natural history such as would have puzzled Agassiz himself; and the question arises, "What shall we do to amuse ourselves this rainy evening?" But "Pat," the engineer, oiler of the domestic machinery of the establishment, and keeper of this menagerie, seems overcome with fatigue; the Astronomer is eclipsed in a corner; the professors are absorbed in sines and co-sines; the Fisherman nods over his paper; Grandma knits her brows and the stocking; Elsie is deep in a book; and no one displays any special interest in the matter until pencils and paper are distributed for the game of Crambo. The *modus operandi* of that most wise and learned game is as follows: Four slips of paper are given each person, on one of which he is requested to write a question, and on each of the other scraps a word. These are then shuffled, and all in turn draw. And now there is great commotion, for each participant is expected to answer his question in rhyme, and to bring the three words which he has drawn, into his answer, also. Such a chorus of "Oh dears," and such dismayed faces! The student proposes to procure the coffee-mill to assist him in grinding out his "pome;" the tennis-player wishes she had a hatchet to chop up a long word which has fallen to her lot, so that she can put it in proper metre; but Mr. Short (6 ft. 2 in.), with watch in hand, calls "Time," and then "Silence," as pencils race over papers as if on a wager. Ten minutes is the brief space allotted for the production of the wondrous effusions; and when Mr. S. announces, "Time's up," the hat is again full; and one says, with a sigh of relief, "There, I never made two lines rhyme in my life before;" another modestly remarks, "You need n't think we are verdant because we are in Green —" but the warning finger of the Philosopher is raised, and Pat, the reader, begins, emphasizing the words drawn as he reads: —

> "Why so much quarrelling about Religion?
> It's as plain as string *beans*
> That from this very means
> The world is not right;
> If I had but clear sight
> I might *hope* ere this night
> Is *beginning* to wane
> The thing to explain.
> But, lacking the wit,
> I must e'en submit
> This doggerel rhyme
> And hope 't is in time."

"Oh! oh!" exclaimed the "small specimen" (aged ten), "that's Grandma's; I heard her say she 'knows beans,' 'cause she is a Yankee;" but the S. S. subsides on hearing the next paper read, and shows so plainly that she "wishes herself further" that it is not difficult to guess the author: —

> "What's quicker than lightning?
> A *Turkey* or a squirrel
> Can 'cut' like a *knife*
> But I never saw a creature rush
> Like a *deer* in all my life."

"Good for Ten-year-old!" exclaim the chorus; and the S. S., brightening up, concludes she'll try it again sometime. Next comes the question: —

> "Where do cabbages come from?
> My will is good, and I *propose*
> To tell you all I can.
> In this dry time a garden hose
> Must come into the plan.
> First plant the seed, and in due course
> Will little shoots appear,
> When each from other has *divorce*
> They'll flourish, it is clear.

> If this rhyme is worth preserving,
> With *mucilage* it may be fixed
> On any wall deserving
> Such wit and wisdom mixed."

As it is well known that the natives of the Emerald Isle have a predilection for cabbages, it is unanimously decided that none but Pat could have perpetrated this; so Pat grins, suggests that a bill poster be secured at once, and proceeds: —

> "How would you like to be a cat?
> In *Timbuctoo* each stern ascetic,
> Though blind to folly as a bat,
> Revels in love *peripatetic*
> Which makes him nimble as a cat.
> But though I'm fond of such agility,
> I better like the busy bees,
> For they display so much ability
> They 'mind one of the *Portuguese*."

At this implied compliment to his people, the black eyes of the foreign student flash approval; and the Mathematician speaks up, saying, "That is the Philosopher, sure, and proves the truth of the saying, 'A little nonsense now and then is relished by the wisest men.'" The

Philosopher smiles benignantly, but does not deny the charge; and the reader continues: —

> "What do you think of the Ornithorhynchus?
> My brain's in a 'muss'
> From thinking of this '*cuss*'
> (Excuse me for using such a word).
> If it lived at *Nahant*
> With this heat it would pant,
> For surely 't is a curious bird.
> You may think me a 'muff,'
> And declare I talk stuff,
> But I hope you'll not doubt my word.
> For though out in all weathers
> Its coat's not of feathers
> But of fur; — at least so I've heard.
> But 'by this *illumination*'
> (Kant's ratiocination?)
> 'I don't see it,' though it may seem quite absurd."

The company, strange to say, hit upon Elsie for this, and are evidently surprised that one so given up to pomps and vanities should display such knowledge of natural history; but they evidently suspect her of shining by reflected light, as she sits next to the Philosopher; and I heard her ask him a question about this animal with the jaw-breaking name. By this time the party have become so brilliant, having polished each other up as by diamond cutters' wheels, that it is "moved and seconded" that we "try again." The laughter has brought down the Chemist from the laboratory, the Fisherman from his den; besides rousing the Astronomer, who scintillates in the corner to such a degree that all others expect to be totally eclipsed. This time the Fisherman, who is also an amateur gardener and farmer on a small scale, draws an appropriate question, in regard to which he enlightens us as follows; and what he says must be true, as we know he has had experience with pigs and hens: —

"Which knows most, a pig or a hen?
'T is hard to tell in rustic *rhyme*
What pigs or hens may know.
A cabbage-head in olden time
Sure knew enough to grow.
If *Balm* and corn to them were thrown
By *parsimonious* Bill
I think the fact would then be shown,
For Piggy'd eat his fill."

Next comes the Chemist with the question: —

"Do you like peanuts?
Peanuts are *double*,

> And so is the trouble
> Involved in *effort*
> To answer it.
> Hand over a few,
> And see if I do
> Not like peanuts
> Better than *Sanskrit*."

Any one who had heard the Chemist warbling, —

> "He who hath good peanuts and gives his neighbor none,
> He sha'n't have any of my peanuts when his peanuts are gone,"

would not have doubted this.

The Philosopher next airs his learning in the following: —

> "What do you admire in a fool?
> Water has such *combustibility*
> That one may rightfully admire
> The happy lack of wise ability
> Which never rivers sets on fire.
> *Truth* needs no *recapitulation*
> To make what's simple plainer still.
> Folly courts our admiration
> Wherever Fashion has her will."

Part of this is so abstruse that I fear the company do not fully appreciate it; so the next is quite startling; and after hearing it we learn the cause of the Astronomer's silent merriment in the corner, and rejoice that Dr. Holmes's experience in "writing as funny as he could" has proved a warning to this individual: —

> "What is stronger than an onion?
> Oh, *scissors!* on a summer night
> To tax a fat *republican*
> In thinking out with all his might
> Some mightier thing than on-i-on.
> Garlic, maybe's not strong enough
> Well, I'll exert my '*spunk*'
> So here you have it, 'in the rough,' —
> A pole-cat, alias s—k."

The Oleaginous Personage comes next with the question, "Do you like Crambo?" which was answered, rather ambiguously, thus: —

> "If our last lingo was a *specimen*
> Of this most wise and learned game,
> 'T is sure that thus not many men
> Would long be known to fame.
> Any of you as well as I
> Would knock our type all into *Pi*,
> If *ghost*, or man, or printer's devil
> Should show us up for good or evil."

Here the sedate and dignified Elsie gives her opinion of a summer recreation after this fashion: —

> "Are you fond of fishing?
> A foolish amusement, it seems to me,
> To be rocking about on the briny sea
> Watching for bites 'neath a broiling sun,
> (Mosquitoes will give you 'em when day is done)
> For my part I'd rather be left in *peace*
> To read of travels in sunny Greece
> Varied by poem on 'Pleasures of *Hope*;'
> — Whate'er my employment I shall not mope —
> But it proves great sport for cousin *Bill*.
> (He's a youth just starting up Life's hill)
> But should he as old as I become
> He would conclude that 't is all a 'hum.'"

Where a person generally considered "proper" became familiar with slang I cannot imagine, but I make no remarks. Owing to the absence of two members of the household, who, having been caught out in the shower, are probably calculating the specific gravity of rain-drops and their effect on new straw hats, we have doubtless been deprived of more poems of surprising depth and brilliancy. And, from regard for the excessive modesty of other participants in the game, I suppress many compositions of rare merit which were brought out this stormy evening. This letter is merely to acquaint you with an important fact, which is as follows. As Dr. Holmes has informed you with regard to the "Asylum for Decayed Punsters," be it known hereby that we have here started a rival institution, — a school for poets; so when you wish to secure the services of any of the graduates, you may know where to apply. And the reason why the game of Crambo is like night is, because it is quiet in the middle and noisy at both ends.

INDEX.

INDEX.

	PAGE
ABBÉ RAYNAL	172
Abbé Ségoigne	172
Acadia, derivation of name	12
" limits of region known as	36
" ceded to England	140
Acadians, banishment of	140
" exempted from bearing arms against France	140
" modern	162–173
" relics of	66–71
Admiralty House	126, 127
Advocate Harbor	30
Almshouse, Philadelphia, old Friends'	38
Amazon River, tidal wave of	27
Amusements for rainy days	194, 195, 198–206
Anemone Cave	190
Annapolis	61–110
" Apostle Spoons	71–74
" " anecdotes of and quotations referring to	74–76
" appearance of town	61, 62
" apple crop	93
" Argall's incursion	50, 51
" Basin	105, 113, 166
" bells, tradition of	68
" block-house	63
" cemetery	76
" church services	92
" climate	82, 83
" fort, history of	55–57
" " at present	61, 62
" people, summer guests, etc.	81, 82
" poem of 1720	99–102

	PAGE
Annapolis River, currents and tide of	85
" romance, a bit of	77–81
" window gardening	103
Argall's incursions	50, 51, 192
Argyle Bay	174
BAIE FRANÇOISE	17
" Fond de la	17
" Ste. Marie	155
Banishment of Acadians or Neutrals	140
Baptism of Indians at Annapolis	49
Baptismal customs, ancient	73
Basin, Annapolis	105, 113, 166
" Minas	22, 29
Basque fishermen	167
Bay, Argyle	174
Bay of Fundy	15, 17, 19, 20
" " " passage across	179
" " " tidal line in water	179
" Shore excursion	104
Beau-Séjour	143
Bell metal	70
" "Carolus" of Antwerp	70
" founders of Belgium	70
Bells	68, 69
Block-house, Annapolis	62
" " Winslow, Me.	63
Blomidon, minerals of	30
Blomidon Cape, legend of	31
Bon Temps, L'Ordre de	45, 46
Bore	19–21
Breton fishermen	167
Brook, Frenchman's	67
"Buckboard"	186
CAJEANS	148
Canoing	186

INDEX.

	PAGE
Cape Breton Island, fortifications of	141, 142
Cape Blomidon	30
" Chignecto	30
" Sharp	34
" Split	35
" d'Or	30
Cave, Anemone	190
Champlain, Samuel de	173
Channel, St. George's	166
Citadel, Halifax	127–131
Clare	153–180
" characteristics of people	162
" church service	160
" convent	163
" costume	161, 162
" customs, etc.	173
" furniture, peculiar house	162
" pronunciation	172, 173
Cod Banks, Newfoundland	167
D'Aulnay	53
De Monts, Pierre du Guast, Sieur de	35–48
" Henry IV. grants title to	36
" arrival of in Acadia	40, 174
" captures Rossignol	41
" in St. Mary's Bay	41, 155
" returns to France	45
" returns to Port Royal with supplies	47
" reception of, by colonists	47
" relinquishes right to Acadia, returning to France	48
De Poutrincourt	48
De Ramezay	57
De Razilly	53
Desert, Mt.	183–195
Deserts, Monts, l'Isle des	183–195
Digby	113–120
" Gap	105, 178, 179
" " rock formations in	178, 179
" herring	117
" Neck	166
" restaurants, odd little	117

	PAGE
Dikes of Équille	94
" " Grand Pré	137
Duvivier	56
Eagre	21
Early fishers on coasts of Nova Scotia and Newfoundland	167
England, treaty between France and	53
English attacks on Port Royal	55, 56
Episode of De Monts's sojourn in St. Mary's Bay	166, 167
Epitaphs, peculiar	76, 119
Équille, description of	85
" significance of name	85
" tidal effects on	85
Eucharistic implements and customs	73
Evangeline, a modern	156, 157, 160
" different representations of	96, 97
"Evangeline," quotations from	11, 22, 37, 38, 66, 70, 80, 91, 96, 97, 131, 136, 137, 139, 140, 141, 146, 148, 153, 154, 160, 165, 170, 171, 176
" what led to the writing of	148, 149
Farms, modern Acadian	168
Fernald's Point	192
Festival, village	177, 178
Feud of De Razilly's lieutenants	53
Fishers on Nova Scotia coast, ancient	167
Fishing, Annapolis and Digby	116, 117
Five Islands	30
Forest fires	107, 108
Fort, Annapolis	55, 57, 61, 62
" Beau-Séjour	143
" Gaspereau	143
" Louisburg	141, 142
French dominions	141
" dike made by	137
" well " "	137
" Neutrals in Philadelphia	39
" " banishment of	140
" settlement, Mt. Desert	192

INDEX. 213

	PAGE
French settlement, Mt. Desert, destruction of	51, 192
Frenchman's Brook	67
Friends' Almshouse	38
Fundy, etymology of	19
" tides of	20
Games	194, 195, 198–206
Gap, Digby	105, 178, 179
Gaspereau, Fort	143
" valley	138
Gheyn, van den (bell founder)	70
Gibraltar of America	142
Glooscap, Indian giant	31
Grand Pré	135–150
" " coffin	135
" " dike	137
" " house, priest's, site of	136
" " smithy, site of	136
" " well	137
Grant of Acadia	51
" " Virginia	51
Granville ferry	86, 87
" Lower (old cannon)	106
Great Head	190
Green Mountain	190, 191
Guast, Pierre du	36
Guercheville, Mme. de	49
Halifax	123–131
" Admiralty House	126, 127
" Arm, North West	131
" books, interesting	126
" churches	126
" citadel	127–131
" en route to	123
" gardens	126
" Harbor	130
" Parliament Building	125
" Point Pleasant	130
Harbor, Advocate	30
" Halifax	130
Havre du Saint Sauveur	193
Hemony (bell founder of Belgium)	70
Henry IV. of France	36
Historical references, Port Royal and Annapolis	40–57

	PAGE
Hooghly River, tidal wave of	20
Hospitality, 71, 86, 87, 104, 105, 124,	170
Incursions of Argall	50, 51
Indian baptism, Annapolis	49
" giant, legend of	31
" settlement on Équille	108
Island, Long	166
" Partridge	30
Islands, Five	30
Jesuits sent to Port Royal	49
" found colony at Mt. Desert	49
Joggin, the	116
Jotun	21
King's decree announced to Neutrals	136, 137, 140
Kings and nobles patrons of bell founders	70
La Havre du Saint Sauveur	193
Lake La Rose	106
Lake Rossignol	41
Laloutre	56
La Rochelle	147
La Tour	53–55
Latten ware	75
Le Borgne	55
Legend of Blomidon	31
" " owls and loons	33
Lescarbot	47
Limits of Acadia	50
" Virginia	51
L'Isle des Monts Deserts	183–195
Logging-camp life	115
Long Island	166
Loons, Indian legend of	33
L'Ordre de Bon Temps	45, 46
Louisburg	141, 142
Mackenzie road	106
Mackerouse	173

214 INDEX.

	PAGE
Mary's Bay, St.	155
Membertou	110
Minas Basin	22–29
Moncton, Bore at	21
Moncton, General	143
Monts, De	36–48
Monts Deserts, l'Isle des	183–195
Mt. Desert	183–195
Mountain, Green	190, 191
NEUTRALS, French, in Philadelphia	39
" in Massachusetts and Louisiana	147, 148
" history of	140
Newfoundland Cod Banks	167
Number of Acadians banished	150
Norman fishers	167
North West Arm, Halifax Harbor	131
OATH of King George	140
Ocgir	21
Odin	21
Old cannon of Lower Granville	106
" cemetery, Annapolis	76
" French dike, Grand Pré	137
" " well " "	137
" " song	157
" poem	99–102
" soldiers' tales	64, 65
Or, Cape d'	80
Ordre de Bon Temps	45, 46
Owls, Indian belief about cry of	33
Ox-yokes, peculiar	168
PARKER'S MOUNTAIN	106
Parliament Building, Halifax	125
Passage, Grand	165
" Petit	165
Phipps, Sir Wm.	55
Pisiquid (Windsor)	144
Point Pleasant, Halifax	130
Poitou	147
Port Royal	45–56
Portuguese fishermen	167
Poutrincourt, De	48

	PAGE
Priest, Indian's trick on	50
Primitive railroad	24
Prince Edward Island	143
RECEPTION of De Monts by colonists	47
Records of Acadians (in Boston)	147
Relics, Annapolis	66–71
Rifle Brigade, Annapolis	57
"Rocking"	188
Rossignol	41
Royal, Port	45–56
SACRAMENTAL customs	73
Saintonge	147
Scandinavian mythology	21
Ségoigne	172
Séjour, Beau, Fort	143
Service, church, at coast settlement	162
Settlers of Minas Basin	145
Shakspeare, anecdote of	74
Sharp, Cape	34
Siege of Louisburg	142
Sieur de Monts	36–48
Song, old French	157
Sound, Somes	191
Split, Cape	34
State in Schuylkill Club	110
St. George's Channel	166
St. John	179, 180
"St. John, 1647," part of Whittier's poem	54
St. John's Island	148
St. Mary's Bay	154
" " " ancient voyagers in	167
" " " species of fish in	168
Styx	34
Subercase	55
TAKING life easily	102, 103
Teintang River	20
Tides of Fundy	20
To tempt the taste	88, 89
Tradition of church bells, Annapolis	69

INDEX.

	PAGE
Troubles leading to banishment of Acadians	140
UNIKAS, Great Lake of	32
United States money	91
Utrecht, treaty of	140
VICTORIA Bridge	116
Village festival, coast settlement	137, 138
Villebon, De	55

	PAGE
Voyages, ancient, St. Mary's Bay, etc.	167
WARE, latten	75
Whittier, part of poem	54
Windmills, peculiar	169
Windsor, desolation near	123
" former name	144
Winslow, Me.	63
Wishing rock	93
YARMOUTH	173, 174

University Press: John Wilson & Son, Cambridge.

www.ingramcontent.com/pod-product-compliance
Lightning Source LLC
Chambersburg PA
CBHW021835230426
43669CB00008B/980